Dear Birthmother

We dedicate this book to our children
Stacy, Cara, David, Erik, and Sarah.

Dear Birthmother:
Thank You For Our Baby

by Kathleen Silber and Phylis Speedlin

Third Edition

Corona Publishing Company
1998

Library of Congress Cataloging in Publication Data

Silber, Kathleen, 1943-
    Dear Birthmother.

    Bibliography: p.
    1. Adoption—United States—Miscellanea.
I. Speedlin, Phylis, 1949-   . II. Title.
HV875.S55 1983   362.7'34'0973   83-1918
ISBN 0-931722-19-5

Cover Design by Simply Creative

Printed and bound in the United States of America
20 19 18 17 16 15 14 13 12

Acknowledgments

Writing a book and preparing it for publication is a challenging task. We are grateful to the many adoptive parents and birthparents who repeatedly encouraged us to share our ideas back in the early 80's. Without your support, we might always have been "too busy" to meet the challenge.

Our special thanks to Lorraine Babcock, Michele Myers, and Louise Dillow. You spurred us on with kind words and friendship when we might have liked to stop.

To Gail Myers our appreciation and affection. Your expert criticism was invaluable in all that we attempted. Most importantly, thank you for teaching us that we could be advocates of what we believe.

Our gratitude also goes out to David Bowen, our publisher and friend. You helped transform our ideas and words into the reality of a finished book.

Since *Dear Birthmother's* initial publication in 1982, we have heard from hundreds of birthparents, adoptive parents, adoptees, and adoption professionals, sharing personal stories and thanking us for being "brave enough" to challenge traditional adoption practice and for pioneering a more humane and open form of adoption. We appreciated your feedback over the past decade, each letter or call reminding us of the pain of closed adoption and the power of open adoption. Many of you have told us that *Dear Birthmother* changed your lives (for the better), and that was our hope when we wrote this book. Your letters, and the dramatic movement we have seen in adoption practice around the country, have been wonderfully gratifying.

This revised version of *Dear Birthmother* reflects the changes which have brought open adoption practice into the 1990's and which will bring it into the 21st century. Our special thanks to Patricia Dorner for your help and advice as we prepared this new edition. We also sincerely thank the adoptive parents and birthparents who updated their stories and those who shared new stories.

We especially thank our husbands, Herbert and Richard. Your understanding, patience, and love sustained us during the years we worked on this book.

This is truly the decade of open adoption.

Kathleen and Phylis
January 1998

CONTENTS

Introduction

Dear Reader,

Dear Birthmother, which was initially published in 1982, explores some of the myths in adoption and details the evolution of open adoption, from letter exchanges to face-to-face meetings and ongoing contact. *Dear Birthmother* has had a tremendous effect on adoption practice nationwide, resulting in a significant shift from traditional adoption to open adoption. In 1982 only a handful of agencies practiced open adoption, compared to today when most adoption agencies and intermediaries offer at least some components of open adoption. However, since the initial publication of *Dear Birthmother*, open adoption has also continued to evolve. This book will examine the theoretical basis for open adoption and its evolution. We also refer our reader to a sequel, *Children of Open Adoption*, by Kathleen Silber and Patricia Martinez Dorner (published in 1990), which follows some of the participants in *Dear Birthmother* and which also explores the lifelong impact of open adoption on all parties, particularly the adopted children.

The ideas we hope to share with you in *Dear Birthmother* began to take shape many years ago when one petite and determined young birthmother helped our adoption program take some dramatic steps forward. After writing a letter to the adoptive parents of her child, a practice we had been allowing (but not encouraging) for several years, this birthmother asked the unthinkable question, "Will you ask them to write me back? I want to know what they think about my baby. I want to know if they could possibly love him as much as I do."

In the 1970's, there was almost no such thing as an "open" adoption. Official records were, and still are in most states, sealed by the courts; communication of any sort between birthparents, their offspring, and their adoptive families was discouraged by laymen and professionals alike as "dangerous." But what is an open adoption? What is this thing which was labeled dangerous and unnatural when *Dear Birthmother* was first published in 1982 and which still remains a shocking concept to many people? The answer is so simple it is disarming. "Open" merely refers to open channels of communication between birthparents and adoptive parents. In addition, in open adoption, all of the choices and control are in the hands of the adopting parents and birthparents themselves, rather than the adoption intermediary.

The wisdom of the past dictated that, in matters of adoption, secrecy was of paramount importance; barring emergency medical considerations, there should never be contact between any of the parties involved after the legal relinquishment. For many years there were valid sociological reasons for this rigid standard; in recent years, however, it has become apparent that the traditional "closed" system of adoption is fraught with dangers of its own. In our experience with open adoption, we have found that the exchange of information between birthparents, adoptive parents, and adoptees has eased a great deal of the trauma associated with the closed system. The times have changed, and today people are more satisfied with a process that is founded upon simple openness and honesty rather than an artificially built up emotional mythology.

I am Kathleen Silber. I am the Associate Executive Director of the National Federation for Open Adoption Education and the Independent Adoption Center in Pleasant Hill, CA, but my work in open adoption began in Texas in the 1970's (and my work in traditional adoption began in the 1960's). When we facilitated that first letter exchange, its impact on the people involved was obvious and immediate. I began to question traditional agency practices and my own professional attitudes toward adoption. I knew, of course, that birthmothers were not the "uncaring baby machines" society generally supposed them to be, and yet I had followed the traditional adoption philosophy which demanded that the birthmother be cut off from her child as completely as possible. I had seen the fear felt by adoptive parents that the birthmother would someday return to snatch up "her" child, and I said "She doesn't want to remember this part of her life; she will forget."

What struck me in watching the first exchanges of letters was how healthy it all seemed—how relieved everyone was. The adoptive parents were relieved to find that among the genes carried by their adopted child, there were none from an uncaring baby machine, and quite happy to hear the birthmother's assurances that she would never invade their lives. The birthmother, in turn, was overjoyed to hear that her child was well loved, happy, and healthy. Now that open adoption has been practiced for many years, we also know that the adopted child is much happier and emotionally more stable knowing that his birthparents had indeed loved him very much (and still love him).

I left Texas in 1986, and I am now associated with another pioneering open adoption agency in California, which offers open adoption with professional counseling, education, and support. There are some distinct differences between agency and independent adoption, as well as differences in the type and quality of adoption services available from one community to the next. However, I encourage all adoption intermediaries—whether they are agencies or independent practitioners—to offer open adoption with comprehensive counseling services and with the control being in the hands of the adoptive parents and birthparents (*not* the intermediary). I also encourage adoptive parents and birthparents to become educated consumers and to seek out adoption programs which offer these essential ingredients.

Since *Dear Birthmother* was originally published I have also evolved in my thinking about open adoption. I am more committed than ever to this practice, which is truly more responsive to people's needs, as well as more honest and humane. I have personally been involved with hundreds of open adoptions, and I have observed that they include a lot of love and caring, rather than fear and mystery which have traditionally surrounded adoption. As a result of my experiences, I advocate meeting in person, sharing full identifying information and engaging in ongoing contact over the years (either through correspondence or in person). I think it is preferable for all parties to have direct access to ongoing contact and to be in control of their lives, rather than at the mercy of laws, agency regulations, or agency personnel (all of which can change over time). I further believe that open adoption is the hope of the future for the field of adoption.

I am Phylis Speedlin. My husband and I adopted our first daughter, Stacy, 13 years ago. Before Stacy's adoption, our opinion of birthparents was ill-defined. Our fantasies about these people ranged from the birthmother being a fertile but uncaring woman to the birthfather being an irresponsible cad. Our most frightening vision was that they both were indecisive about their decision to place Stacy. Could they become villainous kidnappers who would one day reappear to claim their own?

Our thoughts and fears about Stacy's birthparents were not lessened by the circumstances of her adoption. Stacy's placement with us was closed. We lived with ill-founded ideas about her birthmother, as her birthmother undoubtedly lived with incorrect assumptions about herself. By the time we had come to realize from talking to hundreds of adoptees that Stacy would need contact with her birthmother—and, in fact, the birthmother needed contact with Stacy, no matter how remote—the closed system had done its best to complete the closure. When contacted three years after the placement, the pain and guilt that Stacy's birthmother felt over the matter were such that she did not even want to open the letter we sent.

Open adoption became necessary for Stacy soon after her 8th birthday. On the morning of her special day, my husband and I found her in tears before her bathroom mirror. "My birthmother gave me away because she is blond and I am not." The depth of her despair tore our hearts. How could such a beautiful dark-haired girl believe she was rejected because of her looks? Why had none of the information we so freely gave soothed her hurts?

At that time, we sought an intermediary to locate Stacy's birthparents. The adoption agency resisted, but we were protecting our daughter, so we persisted. (I admit our persistence was not without fears because these agency people were the "experts.") Once contacted in person, Stacy's birthmother was at first open and then closed to face-to-face contact with us and/or Stacy.

Our question then became do we persist and approach Stacy's birthfather? Again the agency said "no" and warned us that this would cause serious problems. Stacy, however, was still in pain, and we wanted answers for her. Finally, our intermediary contacted Stacy's birthfather, and it was better than we could have imagined.

Here was a man who had made the decision not to ever move or change his phone number in hopes "one day" his daughter would seek and find him. Through our intermediary, we met Stacy's birthfather—first without Stacy being present. Our meeting confirmed that he loved his daughter and would be good for her.

We also placed Stacy with a child therapist to determine if she could handle an "opening" adoption at the age of 8-1/2 years. After several meetings with the therapist, the day was set—Stacy would meet her birthfather "face-to-face."

How nervous we all were! How Stacy talked and talked, and how her birthfather loved her with his eyes. After that first meeting, Stacy's birthfather seemed to be a natural part of our lives. That first Mother's Day, he sent me a beautiful flower arrangement and said, "Thank you for being Stacy's mom."

Subsequently, on birthdays and at Christmastime, he would come to our home for a short visit. At first, the visits were always with us present. This was to confirm for Stacy that we were and always would be present. She did not have to choose between her adoptive parents and her birthparents.

For Stacy's 12th birthday, however, she asked to go to Sea World in San Antonio with her birthfather and her biological sister. The three of them had a wonderful day.

Regrettably, Stacy's birthmother was never comfortable with open adoption, although she has met Stacy and spoken with her on the phone. I strongly believe that had she been adequately counseled at the time of Stacy's birth, had she known that she did not have to "forget" her child (as society demanded of her), then openness would not pose such a problem for her.

Stacy's sister, Cara, was adopted 11 years ago. By contrast to Stacy, Cara had from her placement a picture of her birthmother, a gift from her birthmother, and a letter telling her how much she was loved and how sorry her birthparents were that circumstances would not allow them to parent her. Within a few years of her placement, Cara's adoption opened further. Phone contact and then a face-to-face "adventure" at Disneyland provided Cara answers to many of her remaining questions. There is no doubt in anyone's mind where Cara gets her physical characteristics and impish personality!

As an adoptive parent, I know that adoption is much more than simply the placement of a long-awaited child. It is a lifetime experience for the adoptive parents, the adoptee, and the birthparents. I am absolutely convinced that for all parties involved, that experience must be open.

This letter from us serves as an introduction to the many beautiful letters included in *Dear Birthmother*. These are the original letters; we have not altered their spelling, grammar, or content in any way. Some letter writers requested that we use their real names, others that we change them; their preferences have been followed.

Our intent when we began to write this book was to share with our readers a sampling of the letters we had seen exchanged through our adoption program. Our goal was to show the warmth, trust, and love possible between birthparents and adoptive parents when given the opportunity to communicate in the form of a letter. In the beginning, these letters were exchanged without any identifying names or addresses, with the agency acting as intermediary. Later, individuals chose to be in direct contact with one another.

Initially, however, many people who read or heard about this form of communication reacted strongly against the idea of even minimal contact between birthparents and adoptive parents. Their reactions could be divided into four typical concerns or assumptions about the adoptive relationship. What surprised us most, though, was that these same four concerns and assumptions seemed to account for much of what we considered our professional attitudes toward adoption and standard agency practices.

As a result of this insight, we redesigned *Dear Birthmother* from a simple collection of letters to include a presentation of the four "myths" (as we now call them) which we had uncovered. It seemed clear that many of the most common emotional problems associated with the closed system of adoption actually stemmed from these myths. Therefore, we wanted to offer solutions, or at least alternatives, to the status quo. The second half of our book evolved during our attempt to arrive at specific recommendations for a myth-free adoption program.

While there have been few long-term psychological studies, we are committed advocates of a new approach to adoption because of the very real benefits it offers in human terms to those personally involved. This new approach includes, as a basic ingredient, open adoption. In 1982, we defined open adoption as any form of communication between birthparents and adoptive parents, either directly or through an intermediary. However, as the practice of open adoption has continued to evolve over the years, so has its definition. Today we distinguish between openness in adoption and open adoption:

Openness in adoption (or semi-open adoption) refers to various forms of communication between birthparents and adoptive parents, such as exchanging letters and pictures, meeting on a first-name-only basis, meeting once but not engaging in ongoing contact, etc. The primary control remains in the hands of the adoption intermediary.
Open adoption includes the birthparents and adoptive parents meeting one another,

sharing full identifying information, and having access to ongoing contact over the years (all three components must occur to fit this definition).* The form of ongoing contact (letters or visitation) and the frequency are determined by the individuals involved in each particular case. In open adoption all of the control and choices are in the hands of the adopting parents and birthparents, rather than the adoption intermediary.

Since this book describes the beginnings and evolution of open adoption, most of the adoptions discussed are semi-open ones. Open adoptions are discussed in the latter part of the book, as well as in *Children of Open Adoption.*

Our experiences have been primarily with infant adoptions and voluntary placements. Although we have not addressed adoptions of older children or involuntary placements, we do feel that open adoption in these situations is also beneficial.

Not every birthparent or adoptive parent will be comfortable with the open practices our work presents. Millions of adoptions have taken place in this country under the closed system, all with the laudable goal of providing homes for children whose birthparents, for one reason or another, could not parent them themselves. It is our fervent wish that *Dear Birthmother* not become a source of guilt or confusion to the birthparents and adoptive parents who have experienced traditional closed adoption. Like most human interactions, adoption is an evolving and dynamic process. As attitudes change and society redefines its value system, what came before is simply history—not something to be denigrated or scoffed at. Given the way our society feels about children today, what would we say to the Victorian lady who gave her children up almost immediately to a wet-nurse, then had them raised by a nanny, then sent them off to a boarding school? She was not evil for doing so—in fact, she was probably trying to be the

---

* Silber, Kathleen and Patricia Martinez Dorner, *Children of Open Adoption*, San Antonio Corona Publishing Co., 1990.

best mother she could be by following what society deemed best for the child. Society now demands openness and honesty in human relationships; we feel that adoption practices should reflect this.

We also advocate open adoption accompanied by comprehensive counseling, educational, and support services. We encourage our reader to seek out an adoption intermediary which offers these essential ingredients to a successful adoption.

The letters published in *Dear Birthmother*, as well as our letter here to you, are based upon the simple concept of open communication and trust. These letters reinforce our commitment to an enlightened adoption process. We invite you to sample these letters and to savor their humanity.

Sincerely,
Kathleen and Phylis

Part One:
Four Myths
Of
Adoption

Until recent years, most adoption agencies and intermediaries followed traditional adoption practices. For birthparents, this meant that the focus of adoption counseling was on the pregnancy and eventual relinquishment of parental rights. Direct interaction with birthmothers and birthfathers revolved primarily around this decision-making process. We did not discuss or prepare these individuals for any aftermath to their decision because we expected our birthparents to go home after terminating their parental rights, forget their untimely pregnancy, and proceed with their own lives.

Our work with adoptive parents also progressed in accordance with professionally approved methods. Applications from prospective adoptive parents were periodically accepted based on the projected availability of infants. If the couple met agency eligibility requirements and passed some initial screening, they were given a formal application for adoption through the agency. Once they completed all necessary paperwork, the couple was assigned a social worker. The social worker would then conduct office interviews and arrange home visits in order to determine the couple's emotional, marital, and financial stability. Their suitability as parents was also evaluated. However, issues the couple would surely face as adoptive parents were not discussed, and birthparents were rarely mentioned. Assuming the couple passed our criteria, they were "approved" and placed on a waiting list—sometimes waiting several years. Eventually a child was placed with them, but this did not signal the end of our involvement. During the statutory waiting period before the adoption could be legally finalized in court, the social worker again visited the couple's home, this time to determine how they were doing as parents. With the final court appearance, our involvement did end. Court records were sealed, our extensive agency files were closed, and we assumed the new family would "live happily ever after."

What we failed to realize was that the standards for our birthparent and adoptive parent programs stemmed from a series of stereotypical misconceptions that have historically surrounded adoption. Today, we are acutely aware of how four such stereotypes persist and dominate adoption practices. We refer to these stereotypes as the four myths of adoption. They represent impressions and assumptions formed partly from media influences, and partly from half-remembered, indifferently accurate, and ambiguously reported stories. Regrettably, these fictions are persuasive, easily understood, and easily passed along. You, as our reader, may cringe as you read indictments against your own attitudes about the people who play out the adoption story.

The four myths of adoption are:

1. **"The birthmother obviously doesn't care about her child or she wouldn't have given him away."**

2. **"Secrecy in every phase of the adoption process is necessary to protect all parties."**

3. **"Both the birthmother and birthfather will forget about their unwanted child."**

4. **"If the adoptee really loved his adoptive family, he would not have to search for his birthparents."**

In the next four chapters we will explore with you the awesome influence that each myth has on adoption. We offer you our experiences and evolution, and the poignant thoughts and reactions of people who are living today's adoption drama. You will have the opportunity to see deeply into the lives of birthparents and adoptive parents. Mothers who "give away" a child to another set of parents to nurture can make you weep with the depth of their love—for the child and for the new parents. Adoptive parents who share their infertility experience and grief will deeply touch you even if you think you have no interest in adoption.

Our clients are not all highly educated or insightful. They come from various socio-economic levels. These individuals, in fact, typify the women and men involved with adoption daily throughout the United States—with one exception. Each of our clients has been encouraged to deal with their untimely pregnancy or their infertility in a myth-free manner.

1
Dear Birthmother,
We Know You Care

Myth Number One:
*"The birthmother obviously doesn't
care about her child or she wouldn't
have given him away."*

People accept the first myth of adoption as true because they make the following assumptions about the birthmother:

- She is able to ignore the first stirrings and movements of life within her body.
- She is able to forget the beauty of creation and the actual birth experience.
- She is able to disregard the sight of a beautiful new-born baby.
- She is able to suppress the innate yearnings to nurture her child.
- She is able to dismiss the fantasies, hopes, and dreams she may have had for her child's future with her.
- She is able to ignore the pain of signing a relinquishment document, knowing that all her legal rights to her child are forever terminated, and that she has sealed her child's future for better or for worse.

Until you meet someone like Lindy, you can more readily accept such assumptions and believe that birthmothers do not care about the life they can "so easily" give away. Lindy was a young woman four months pregnant when we first met her. The months of pregnancy had emotionally drained Lindy because she loved the little life growing and moving within her body. Throughout her pregnancy, Lindy struggled with her own feelings and the conflicting pressures of family members. The day her son, Noah, was born, Lindy felt true joy at seeing him alive and healthy, and hearing his first cry. She protectively cared for Noah during her three-day hospital stay, and then arranged a unique religious service to be held in the hospital chapel. The service was held on the day Lindy last saw Noah, to bless him and his future with his "new parents." That service was Lindy's special goodbye.

Certainly, Lindy's actions cannot be described as irresponsible or uncaring. She, in fact, struggled for nine months to come to terms with Noah's existence separate from hers. It took all her courage to sign the relinquishment papers that placed her son for adoption.

The depth of Lindy's love for Noah and the conscientiousness of her decision is best reflected in this letter, written to her son shortly after birth:

> To a very special boy,
>
> I don't quite know how to begin this letter, except to say that I love you very, very much.
>
> I will try to write this letter so that you will understand fully the reasons I chose adoption for you.
>
> I was 19 at the time you were conceived. I was very young and disillusioned about love. I was going through a hard period in my life. I was not communicating with my parents. So I reached out to whatever love I could find.
>
> I met your father in the summer . . . We dated for about two months and we broke up. After 1-1/2 years, in December we started dating again.
>
> I was really having problems with my parents so I moved in with your father. I was very much in love with your father. Your father and I were different in many ways. We had different ideas about love, and after 5-1/2 months I moved home to my parents. Shortly after, I discovered I was pregnant. I can hardly describe my feelings. I was filled with joy and sorrow.

I was so happy to be carrying you, and I was sad because your father was involved with someone else. I told your father about you and we talked and decided that marriage would not be fair to anyone, especially you.

After I told my parents (your birthgrandparents) they were deeply hurt. They are very old fashioned and religious. After much discussion we all agreed that I should go to live with my sister 1200 miles away.

As I approached the mid-term of my pregnancy, I was faced with the fact of how to raise you. I wanted so badly to keep you and protect you, but the fact that I had no money, no job, and no place to live, I decided for adoption. No matter how dearly I love you, I was going to have to choose adoption so that you could live a full and happy life. That's all I wanted, was for you to be happy and to have so many things I couldn't provide. I couldn't live with myself, if I weren't able to give you everything you need and want. So you see, adoption was the right choice. You have a loving family and two beautiful parents who love and adore you as much as I do.

If you were able to live on love, there would be no problem. Because I have so much love in my heart for you, you'll never know. But you're not able to live on love alone, and as much as it hurts me to admit it, that is all I could have gave you. It's just not enough. But I wish it was. There was no reason for you to suffer because of my selfishness. Try to understand I did it because I love you so very much.

As time went by I got very fat! And on March 26, at 6:25 P.M. I delivered the most beautiful 6 lb. 7 oz. baby boy. I was so proud and I was filled with joy. You were so tiny and beautiful. I couldn't believe I had given birth to such a beautiful and perfect little boy. I thank God every day for you. I am still proud of you and think of you every single day. I wonder what you're doing and what you look like.

I stayed at the hospital for three days. During my stay I fed you, held you, and prayed for you. I'll never forget the first time I held you. You threw up all over me. HA-HA! But it was O.K. You could really make some funny faces. I took dozens of pictures. You were so cute! The day finally came (too quick) for me to go home. On March 29th I signed relinquishment papers, giving you the right to a full and happy life. It was the hardest thing I've ever done.

We held a special service for you in the chapel of the hospital. A friend bought a gown for you, and a bonnet and we dressed you up and we all prayed that you would have the life you deserved. You were so beautiful in that gown. So fragile and pure. I love you.

As I saw you for the last time I realized I should not be sad, but be thankful that you have two beautiful parents that love and adore you very much. I know that you will bring them an unmeasurable amount of joy and happiness.

I hope this letter will clear up any doubts of my love for you, or any questions you might have. I would like you to know that if you ever decide to try and find me, please do!! I'll be waiting anxiously if you ever decide to. It would be a dream come true. But the decision's yours and I'm sure your parents will be open and supportive of any decision you make. If you choose not to see me, I'll try to understand.

I hope I've said the right thing to make you realize I really do love you! You've brought me so much happiness that I can't even describe. I hope someday that I'll be able to bring you happiness by being your friend. Please understand that I don't want to interfere in your life, or come between you and your parents. I don't want to be a threat to your relationship with your parents.

I know this letter is probably going to be a

shock. I don't want to hurt you. I just want to love you, and I do with all my heart. If and when you decide to see me, please talk openly with your parents. Get their opinion.

But whatever happens, know that I will always be here, forever.

As I come to a close, I realize that this may be the last time I'll ever be able to express my feelings to you, so once again I'll say I'll be here forever and ever. I love you so very, very much. Never forget that.

God bless you and your adoptive parents. I love you all very much.

Love,
Your Birthmother
Lindy

As her letter illustrates, Lindy was not able to ignore the fact that she had created life or to forget the experience of nurturing her "beautiful and perfect little boy." Contrary to the first myth, she responded to her pregnancy and to Noah with deep maternal feelings. Lindy's decision to place Noah for adoption does not somehow magically erase those feelings.

Lindy wrote a second letter to Noah's new parents four months after Noah's birth. This second letter by Lindy shows just how unselfish and painful the decision of adoption can be for a birthmother:

Dear Patti and John,

Over the past few months I've been trying to figure out what to write. First of all I'd like to thank you for giving Noah a loving home. I'm sure he will bring great happiness and joy to you in the years to come.

You both know a little about my family. I'm the baby of six. There are 5 girls and 1 boy. As you already know, my real father died when I was very young. I don't remember him at all. I was brought up by a wonderful step-father, who I consider as my real father. My father was very protective of me.

And as I grew older it was hard for him to accept the fact that his little girl was growing up. Like most teenagers I went through a period of rebellion. I fought with my parents, and I lost all communication I had with them.

After my 19th birthday, I moved out of my parents' house and moved in with my baby's father. We both had different ideas about love and to say the least, our love didn't last very long.

After 5 months, I moved back to my parents house. I soon discovered I was pregnant. It hit me hard. I had mixed emotions about my pregnancy.

After much thought and discussion, I decided for adoption. There's so much I want Noah to have that I can't provide like a stable home life. I want you to know I feel very secure about my decision.

I'll tell you a little bit about my pregnancy. First of all I got very fat! HA-HA! I had morning sickness a lot. I also was very content in bringing this child to you. At times I feel sad, but then I think about the love he's giving and receiving. Deep in my heart I know he's getting all the love that two people can give. I have peace inside knowing Noah is with a real family.

There is one thing I feel I must tell you. I was never very close to my parents, so I ask you to always be open and honest with him. Never lose communication with him. I never realized how important that was until I lost what little communication I had. I know now, because I learned the hard way.

I hope you'll respond to this letter and if it's not too much to ask, could you please send me a picture. I would really appreciate it.

I'd like to thank you for the chance to express my feelings. I am really grateful and I want you to know that even though we've never met, you both have very special places in my heart. You always will.

Thank you again for giving Noah all your love.

Please write back and send a picture.
I Love You! Here's a picture of the last time
I saw him!

Lindy

P.S. Did you get his bonnet and poem?

Lindy's decision to choose adoption for Noah, like count-less similar decisions by other birthmothers, was motivated by love: "I want the best for my child and I cannot now give him that!" The hope for a better life is not the motivation of a person who does not care. Why, then, the first myth?

We believe that the simple answer lies in the generally held notion that one cannot be biologically responsible for a child's life and make a logical decision not to parent that child. Conceiving and then giving birth "naturally" mandates at least eighteen years of daily parental responsibility, or so we have been taught. To break this pattern by not assuming the parental role is to be unnatural about something we hold very dear—our families. Therefore, to protect the family unit and the socially accepted order of things, birthmothers who place their children in surrogate homes are conveniently clas-sified as unfeeling and uncaring—like fertile baby machines.

Other influences also maintain the uncaring myth. Adoptive parents, coming from a perspective of imposed childlessness, find it especially difficult to understand the act of giving away a baby. In addition, many individuals still believe that bearing a child outside the sanctions of marriage is a shameful and unspeakable event. Their collective attitude toward the birthmother ranges from superiority to condemna-tion to punishment.

One birthmother still vividly remembers the emotional aftermath of seeing her newborn son. After being with him for about three hours, she returned her baby to the nurse know-ing that would be the last time she would see him. She began to cry, "I cried all the tears that I will ever cry in my life in the hours after that. I cried long and hard." This birthmother asked then to see a minister, thinking that in some way he would be a comfort to her. The minister who responded to this tearful young woman proceeded to tell her what a terrible person she was. "You deserve the pain and agony you are feeling, and I am glad you realize that," he said.

In summary, believers of the first adoption myth label a birthmother as uncaring in order to explain her unnatural act, then justify condemning her by the righteous stance that, after all, nice girls would not do such things. If a nice girl would not or could not give away her child, then one may dismiss or punish this birthmother. One of the cruelest but most typical forms of punishment is forever denying the birthmother information about her child. "She does not deserve any information; she gave away all her rights," is the most common stance.

As you read the next letter, consider that this is a birthmother you may have heard about, or thought or spoken about in terms of the uncaring myth. Her letter, by contrast, reflects that the relinquishment of her son was accomplished only after careful and painstaking plans, not unthinking abandonment:

Dear Friends,

Another year has come and gone and Robert must be becoming a beautiful young man. At this hour exactly two years ago, joy came to my life and although you wouldn't know for several days, it also came to yours. Of course I always think of Robert and wish him well, but today especially, I am filled with warmth and love. I have read and heard of the longing and void most birth mothers feel on their child's birthday, and I must admit that I felt the same way last year at this time, but this year the feeling has blossomed to pride. It feels wonderful knowing that our son has experienced another year, and know that the new year holds growth and happiness not only for him, but for you.

It is a great coincidence that the time of Robert's birthday fell so near to the time of my reading of a book called "The Adoption Triangle." It is a well put-together book, and I found it most interesting and informative. I read that most adoptive parents are only willing to accept healthy babies, whereas natural parents simply accept what they receive. Your wanting, accepting, and most importantly loving of Robert with the knowledge that he may have had a congenital disease really raises the respect that I feel for you. That is not the love adoptive parents give, but the love the real parents give.

I also read of the doubts and fears felt by birth parents, adoptees and adoptive parents. I guess that I am different because these are not the emotions which I have. I have always tried to express to you with openness, the loyalty and friendship which I have for you. I feel confident knowing that you will be open with Robert and that he can be honest with you. Don't ask me how I know, I just know. I do feel close to your family, and hope that you feel close to me.

The only new news that I have to relay is not of me, but of Robert's father, John. He and his wife are now expecting their second child. I do not know whether they are hoping for another boy or if they want a girl this time, but I do know that he will be happy with any child, and still be a wonderful father.

I must close for now, but not short of wishing your family all that's best and wishing Robert a very happy birthday.

Lovingly,
Lana

For us, the first myth of adoption is a troubling paradox. We know birthmothers like Lana relinquish their parental role and their legal rights because they want to give their child what they know he or she needs and what they think they can not provide at that time—love, care, and security from two parents in a normal home situation. Yet these birthmothers who make careful and unselfish decisions are condemned and punished. Must they choose to raise their child themselves to avoid a lifetime of living with the first myth?

Birthmothers (especially teenagers) who experience an unplanned pregnancy are told by family members, social workers, and other adoption intermediaries about the wisdom of placing their child for adoption: "If you really loved your unborn child, you would make the responsible decision to place your child for adoption in a loving home with two parents." The typical counseling program for the birthmother when she is weighing her options emphasizes that if she chooses adoption she will be thinking, not of herself, but of "the welfare of her child."

Once legal relinquishment papers are signed, however, the same counselor may begin to practice behavior spelled out in the myth. The birthmother's responsible decision has somehow become "uncaring," an act of "abandonment," or a "failure as a person and as a parent." The paradox is emphasized every time post-placement counseling for the birthmother is brief or nonexistent, although the counseling during the decision-making process had been intense. This sudden switch in attitudes is viewed by the birthmother as a rejection of her and her decision, resulting in unnecessary confusion, unresolved feelings, and lingering doubts.

Our contact with birthmothers has dramatically convinced us that these women are not "unfeeling baby machines." A birthmother merely chooses to bring her child into this world, rather than abort it, and then to place that child in a home with two people who will nurture, guide, and assist the child to become an adult. As one birthmother wrote:

> . . . I had rather given Cara life than to go through with an abortion. The thought entered my mind that I could make a couple very happy. At the same time go on with my life. Also giving her a chance to live and grow up on God's Earth as a Human Being. And a beautiful one at that. Believe me it would of hurt me worse if I'd had an abortion. So instead I made four wonderful people happy, including myself....

Does this birthmother merit being labeled uncaring by our society by participating in another act—the act of abortion—which she dreads even more? Certainly we do not believe she has earned the badge of an uncaring person because she chose adoption as her best alternative. Nor does this birthmother merit the punishment of forever being denied simple information about her daughter. We think such punishment far exceeds any possible crime.

Since we have rejected the fiction that birthmothers are uncaring individuals, our work must deal with the depth and variety of their emotions—emotions that remain long after relinquishment papers are signed. Letters provide an avenue for communication, as well as a familiar format that both writer and receiver are comfortable using and handling.

Letter writing by birthmothers is helpful for them to come to grips with their decision. Their letters serve as concrete emotional outlets for feelings about the child's physical separation. By putting words on paper, a birthmother is forced to focus on the reality of her decision. A letter may be her best first step in healing and moving forward.

Tina, a nineteen-year-old birthmother, wrote her newborn son the day she was to leave the hospital. Tina had cared for him throughout the hospital stay and her goodbye to him is clearly painful:

> My Dearest Son,
>
> It's so hard for me to start this letter. I have so many things I would like to explain. But I am not quite sure where to begin. I do want you to remember that every decision I've made concerning you, was made out of love. And with only your best interest at heart. I only hope that you realize that my placing you for adoption doesn't mean I don't love you. Although it was hard for me to let you go I know I made the right choice. Remember I love you, I will always love and care for you. Nothing will ever change that.
>
> Let me first explain the relationship between your birthfather and me. I met your birthfather at

a very vulnerable time in my life. You birthfather was also going thru rough times. We met one another when we needed each other the most. Together we loved and shared many special moments together. Sometimes during those special moments something beautiful happens. As did in our case. That something beautiful was you. But unfortunately the time we shared and the love we felt was only temporary. There wasn't enough to build a life time on. I wish things could have been different. But I don't regret what happened. I am so happy, so happy to have been apart of your creation.

When I looked at you, all the time we were in the hospital, I think you will look a lot like me. I really cannot see much of your birthfather in you right now. I am sure time will change all that. I do know that you were the most beautiful baby I had ever seen. From the moment you were born, you had such a wonderful color, such rosey chubby cheeks, and the cutest facial expressions I had ever seen. The whole time I spent with you, you were so good. Whenever I went to the nursery to see you all the other babies would be crying, but you were so content. You never cried or complained. When it came time for your feeding and I would take you in my arms, you never seemed like you wanted to eat, just sleep. I am afraid you got your desire to sleep from me. I love to sleep.

Now because I am your birthmother, I wanted nothing but the best for you. <u>I had to think of your life, separate from mine.</u> I gave you life and in giving you life, I also had the responsibility of giving you the best life had to offer. I wanted you to have the best chance to live your life to the fullest. Even if that included living your life without me. That's why I choose adoption. Thru adoption I was able to make sure you had the things I couldn't give you. You needed to be surrounded by the love only a family can bring. To be in a home filled with that love. To be brought up by two people who loved each other, as much as they loved you. Alone I was unable to give you all of this. Adoption is a gift from my heart for you, Son. I wanted you to have the world. I believe with all my heart you now have it. Always remember how lucky you are. You have two parents who love you just as much as I do. And although you don't see me, I will always be with you, my love for you continues everyday of my life. I envy your parents, for they will be with you to share all your ups and downs. But I thank God I was able to have a part in your creation. I thank Him for making it possible to share those first three days with you. For there was never a moment you were not loved. I will always have you in my memories. With that memory goes my undying love.

I realize there's so little time and space to write all the things I wanted to teach and explain to you. I am glad I know your parents will be there to answer and tell you everything you will need to know about life. If I can I'd like to leave you with a thought. I think if you listen and adhere to my advice it will make life and the problems it brings might be a little easier. Son, always <u>respect yourself,</u> and show the same respect you show yourself to every person you meet. Don't ever underestimate yourself or put yourself down, always strive to do the best you can, by all means you can! Everyone is bound to make mistakes. You find out what went wrong and why. You learn from your mistakes, then put it in the past, never dwell on them. Remember you're never alone. There's so many people standing on your side. Always ready and able to help, should you need it. Together with love, you and your family will overcome everything.

Today adoption records are kept closed to the children that are placed for adoption. But even as I write this letter, the laws are changing. I suspect one day the records will be opened and you will be able to locate me. I will always welcome you with love and open arms. I'd like nothing better than to see you. But promise me the decision to find me will be your own. Don't ever let anyone, even me, pressure you into any decision you don't want to make. As long as you're happy, I will be happy. I will understand and accept any decision you make.

Forever, you will remain a part of me. I will always be proud of you, Son. My love always with you.

I pray nothing but good times fill your days and nights.

Good luck in whatever you do.

> Always,
> With All My Love,
> Your Birth Mother
> Tina

Tina's letter is the farewell to her son that is needed for her to begin to fully understand and accept his life separate from hers. Without the letter, Tina might be forced to deal with her son's placement in any of a number of vastly different ways. One birthmother who was denied this type of communication and post-placement support, recalled many years later (at age thirty-five), "After I signed the papers, I hated myself. I started hanging around with people involved in heavy drinking and drugs. I felt like I deserved that. I believe I would be dead or crazy now, if I did not get pregnant and keep my second child." This mother was consumed by a need to punish herself for her uncaring act, and to redo her decision. Sadly, we know many other birthmothers who relate similar dramatic stories that emphasize how their adoption decision traumatizes them for a lifetime.

Tina, by contrast, was allowed to deal with her decision and her loss by communicating her love to her son. Her feelings were not discounted by the counselors who had worked with her, and she was not subtly rejected. Tina was helped to go on with her life without the guilt and pain caused by the myth's sudden condemnation.

Letter exchanges also benefit others in the adoption drama. Adoptive parents are given a unique opportunity to know the birthmother of their child from personal correspondence. This helps erase shadowy stereotypes of those "other parents" that might affect their relationship with their child. Adoptive parents also receive direct information and facts to share with their children rather than innuendo and guesswork when the inevitable questions come. One adoptive mother told us, "I treasure the letters to my sons. They let me off the hook of having the total responsibility of teaching the boys that their birthparents were real people with regular feelings, hopes, and pain."

Adoptees also benefit from the rejection of the first myth through the letter exchanges. In a personal letter, the central question of every adoptee, "How could someone give me away?" is answered by the only person capable of providing an answer. Tina's son, for example, will not be forced to internalize feelings of worthlessness from having been "discarded." Regrettably, much of the pain other adoptees experience will not be lessened. Society's tenacious belief in the first myth will always translate for them as "obviously your birthmother did not and does not care about you."

In order that our rejection of the first myth become more than a hollow protest against a social ill, we have taken steps to change the public's belief in this myth. Foremost among these steps is the letter exchanges which we encourage. Here is a recap of what we are convinced the letters accomplish:

• For birthmothers, letters constructively focus feelings of love and loss.
• For adoptive parents, letters awaken needed empathy and insight.
• For the adoptee, letters answer questions positively.

We hope that the few letters we have shared so far with you, our reader, have encouraged you to question and reject ready assumptions that birthmothers "obviously do not care."

2
Lifting
the Veil of Secrecy

Myth Number Two:
*"Secrecy in every phase of the adoption
process is necessary to protect all parties."*

Secrecy in adoption proceedings continues as today's most persistently practiced myth. Widespread support for anonymity between the participants in adoption remains unquestioned by many adoption agencies, other professional intermediaries, and society in general. In both traditional and semi-open adoption, full identities of the parties involved are not shared. In fairness to the supporters of secrecy, their motivation stems from the desire to protect the adoptive parents, the birthparents, and the child. We are convinced that this desire is misguided.

Adoption was not always a matter of secrecy, nor did laws always seal adoption records. In Colonial days, adoption could be accomplished by merely recording the transfer of a child, much like we now transfer the deed to our homes or title to our cars. Early laws, such as those passed in Texas and Vermont in 1850, were intended to make this type of informal adoption more secure. All court records, however, were open to the public.

The origin of the second myth of adoption and the practice of sealing records has to be understood in the light of a different era, the early 1900s. Social work as a profession was just developing. Unlike today, there were many destitute children available for adoption, but few potential adoptive parents. It was largely believed that such social ills as poverty, sexual promiscuity, alcoholism, and crime were passed on to children in the genes. For that reason middle-class family members feared taking to their hearts a child of questionable parentage. The risk was just too great that the maturing child would exhibit the sinful attributes of the criminal or perverted parents.

In order to sell the public on adoption as a viable means of caring for large numbers of children, social workers needed to establish themselves as experts in matching children to families. They thus assumed the status of a third party between prospective adoptive parents and birthparents. The pressures of trying to recruit adoptive parents led social workers to give assurances that the child was without physical, emotional, or mental defect.

The selling job that this profession mounted involved legislative protection as an essential element. Sealed records evolved, in effect concealing the background of the child. In addition, the child's birth certificate no longer was stamped with the fact of illegitimate birth. Later, replacement birth certificates began to be issued, listing names of the adoptive parents as if the child had been naturally born to them. This practice of issuing new birth certificates was termed a "legal rebirth" for the adoptee. What started as a process to make adoption more attractive and to protect the child from being forever haunted by his illegitimate birth became linked with the idea of rebirth and the mandate of secrecy. By 1950 most states had laws forever sealing original birth certificates and court records, not only from the public but also from the adoptive parents and the adoptee.

Today, adoptive parents in traditional or semi-open adoptions receive selected information both about the child they plan to adopt and about the individuals who gave him life. Selection is made by social workers and other adoption intermediaries who decide which facts to share and which facts are best left secret. This sifting of information invariably weeds out certain factors. Rarely do adoptive parents obtain detailed social histories on both birthparents or their immediate families. Medical histories are provided, but the information revealed is sometimes only oral. Even when written medical histories are provided, adoptive parents must remember that the child's medical background is not "complete," since one's medical history continues to evolve over time. In addition, social realities of the birthparents such as alcohol or drug usage are frequently omitted. One adoption social worker we know believes that the adoptive couple needs "only the positives." This social worker has identified herself with numerous individuals who, possibly unconsciously, harbor the belief that adoptive parents are doing the homeless child a favor. Therefore we still hear, "How wonderful of you to adopt that poor baby!" as if the couple is being courageous and generous.

Secrecy imposed on adoptive parents is also motivated by a desire to protect the infertile couple denied their own natural child. The conventional wisdom of the professional in control of the adoption proceedings is, "The adoptive couple will be happiest if they can be as much like natural parents as possible." This translates to providing the couple with a near-perfect child, securing the same legal status as "real parents," and then helping them forget the different way their family unit was formed. Forgetting is encouraged every time the professional in control decides not to mention the role birthparents may play in the adoptee's future or the unique responsibilities of adoptive parenthood. Some physical likeness between the child and his adoptive parents will help dispel any questions about his origins, and the adoptive parents will be further protected from publicly facing the reality of their childlessness.

Birthparents are also supposedly protected by secrecy of traditional adoption practices. They are essentially told by the professional intermediary, "Give us the baby you have decided to place. Now you can go away and forget this experience; we will protect you." Such protection includes withholding information from them about the adoptive family's physical appearance, interests, or personalities. By denying specific facts about the people who will nurture and guide the adoptee to adulthood, the intermediary assumes birthparents live easier with their decision. Their logic represents the "out of sight, out of mind" philosophy. If the intermediary is progressive and compassionate, birthparents might receive a brief, probably oral, profile of the adoptive family. Interestingly, the adoptive family is almost always described as a "professional family who is financially stable and will provide a loving home."

Finally, the second myth of adoption is designed to protect the adoptee. Although illegitimacy lacks its past shameful connotations, and attitudes toward bringing children of different or "bad" blood into the family are not as prevalent, many individuals believe that secrecy is necessary to hide socially abhorrent elements in the child's background. The goal is to shield the adoptee from the unfavorable information in his own birth history.

Similarly, secrecy in all phases of adoptive practices is used to spare the child the conflict of two sets of parents. The logic here stems from the idea that believing something makes it true. Deny the fact that two caring birthparents exist and they will not exist, especially if the adoptive parents do a good job at parenting. In total, the personal wisdom and persistent mythology of the social worker or other professional intermediary controls the adoptee's future—"some facts are best concealed so that the adoptee-child will be forever protected."

The adoption practices described above result directly from an adherence to the second myth. When we began to question the basis of these practices, we uncovered numerous problems. We discovered that there exist latent messages in the intermediary's selection of information and encouraged forgetting. These messages serve to harm, not protect, the individuals involved in the adoption drama. Adoptive parents, birthparents, and adoptees are actually forced to cope, without recourse or review, with what the intermediary thought was in their best interest.

For adoptive parents, secrecy handicaps their parental role identification. Because the adoptive parents typically are not provided much information about the individuals who gave their child life, birthparents remain shadowy stereotypes. The intermediary message to be as much like natural parents as possible also translates to mean that adoptive parenthood must be second best to the status of a "real parent."

Birthparents are also seriously encumbered by closed

adoption. Denial of information about the adoptive parents prevents them from ever being sure that their decision was right. "Do the adoptive parents love him as much as I do? Is he safe and protected? Is he healthy and happy?" The questions persist for millions of birthparents, but the questions remain unanswered. In addition, the message to the birthparent from the trained intermediary to "try not to think about it" translates to impose a lifetime of shame, for "it" must be a shameful mistake or an unforgivable sin.

Finally, secrecy robs the adoptee of his right to reach his full potential. Instead of his psychological energy being directed to the normal process of growth, the adoptee spends time dwelling on the unanswered questions, "Who are my birthparents?" and "Why am I not with them?"

As with the first myth of adoption, we reject the need for secrecy between members of the adoption drama. Imposed secrecy denies individual choice and robs human potential. It prevents honesty and forces a punitive distance among the five people fate brought together.

Once again, we use letters to bridge the chasm traditionally created by mandatory anonymity. Letters move all participants expectantly toward the benefits only possible through honest and open sharing:

> Dear Birthmother,
>
> I am writing a letter I have wanted to write for three years now. The child you gave birth to just over three years ago is my daughter—Stacy.
>
> The reason I have wanted to write you is because I want you to know that the child you created, nurtured for nine months, gave birth to, and then placed with me is very special. When I look at her beautiful face I think of you and know you must be beautiful. When I am enjoying her gentle, loving nature, I think of you and know you must be gentle. When I get somewhat frightened by her intelligence, I think of you and know you must be bright.
>
> Always know that I am fully aware of the magnitude of the gift you placed with us. I am committed

to Stacy growing up to be a secure and happy woman. I thank you for letting me parent her. I am comfortable as Stacy's mother and I am willing to share with you letters about and pictures of <u>our daughter</u> if and when you would like these.

I have written this letter as one mother to another. My husband is also committed to the offer of communication and certainly to our daughter.

I will write again if you wish. If not, that is okay.

Stacy is well and happy and will grow up a secure and wonderful person.

Love,

Stacy's Mom

The preceding letter was written by Stacy's adoptive mother three years after her adoption. At the time Stacy was adopted, letters were infrequently exchanged because we were still deluded by the second myth. Stacy's adoptive mother, however, felt a strong need to communicate her feelings. "I have needed to tell my child's birthmother these things for a long time," she said. "I'm just glad I could." The letter was delivered by the adoption agency to Stacy's birthmother who eagerly received such unexpected communication. To date Stacy's birthmother has not written a return letter but the bridge for future communication was opened.

Today many adoption intermediaries encourage the exchange of letters and pictures between adoptive parents, birthparents, and their children (and in open adoptions, the exchange of full identifying information and the access to ongoing contact over the years). Picture exchanges include current photographs of the children, the birthparents, and the adoptive parents. Several years ago, most adoption professionals would have never considered such exchanges. We believed secrecy and total anonymity were necessary. Shattering this second myth was more difficult for us than the first because all our training had taught us that our closed methods really did protect our clients. Our belief in this new approach grew stronger, however, with the repeated and sincere excitement of our clients as they received personal information, names, and pictures. Instead of our openness having a chilling effect on the participants in our adoption stories, they began to demand even more openness, and less protective measures. Today our parents seem to accept these exchanges as basic to the adoption process.

Denise, a twenty-seven-year-old adoptive mother describes in the following letter why she does not want a veil of secrecy between her and her son's birthmother:

> To a very special person,
>
> I am writing this letter to a person who has a special place in my heart. You have given me something so precious and special—my son. He is the greatest joy in my life.
>
> This letter is very difficult to write—not because I don't want to—but because I don't have a name to identify you with. What little bit I do know about you makes me feel like we're a lot alike. We seem to have similar interests in hobbies. Even though we've never met I consider you a special type of friend.
>
> We have named our son James. He has to be the most beautiful baby in the world. His features are so perfect. Of course, he is growing in leaps and bounds. All of his baby hair has fallen out and new hair is growing in. I think his hair is going to be brown to match his beautiful <u>huge</u> brown eyes.
>
> I'm not sure if great detail is what you would like to read or not so I'm playing this by ear— here goes.
>
> James is very active and alert. He has been turning from his stomach to back for about two weeks now. It won't be long before he will be sitting alone and crawling. He gets so frustrated when he can't do something but he is persistent. To date, James doesn't have any teeth but he sure is drooling a lot (has been for about 2 months). Ever since James came to us he has been trying to suck his thumb but never could figure out how to hold onto it. Well, he has figured out how and is an avid

thumb sucker. I tried to give him a pacifier but he acted like it was choking him. The only time he really sucks his thumb is when he is tired or sleepy. James sleeping habits are great—he goes to bed (by his choice) at 8:30 p.m. and sleeps until 9 or 10 a.m. He really likes and requires a lot of sleep. James is definitely a little creature of habit, he doesn't take too well to his routine being disrupted. Right now he is going through a stage where he cries at the mere sight of a stranger (even his grandparents). I've been told this is very normal and that he will outgrow it. James tends to be on the serious side. He always looks as if he is in deep thought. He is not very generous with his smiles yet, but when he does smile it's worth the wait. It looks as though he is going to be rather cautious of people until he knows them well—that's good in a way.

I could ramble on for hours but I'm not sure that's a good idea. I feel like you loved James very much and I don't want to cause you any unnecessary pain. I love James more than words on paper can begin to describe. He gives me so much pleasure and has brought joy to everyone in our family. Without you I would not be experiencing such joy and for that I am very grateful to you. I know you will never forget James but I hope you will never worry about him. James has a very loving family and will always be taken care of. I saved all of the background information concerning yourself and James' birthfather. When James is old enough I will give it to him. It is my sincere hope that someday you will feel comfortable in writing James a letter. It will be kept with everything else and given to him later on. If James wishes to locate you when he is of age, I have promised myself to help him in anyway I can. I hope you will be receptive if that search ever takes place.

For now you should concentrate on your future. I know it will be bright and happy. Please

remember that you will always have two anony-
mous friends who think you are very special. You
gave joy to me and my husband by giving life to our
son. We will always be grateful.

God Bless You,
Denise

All members of the adoption drama benefit from lifting
the veil of secrecy. Adoptive parents are not denied information about the individuals who gave their child life.
Stereotypes of the child's birthparents are replaced with
actual facts and personal data about the birthmother and
birthfather. Through individual communication via the letter
exchanges, adoptive parents learn about and empathize with
the birthparents. The insight that develops will be invaluable
to the adoptee as he begins to question his adoptive parents
about his heritage and his birthparents.

Paula and Ken are adoptive parents who were married
four years before they sought adoption to form the family they
wanted. They began adoption proceedings believing birthmothers were probably uncaring and birthfathers irresponsible. They subsequently learned from their birthmother that
neither of these half-formed stereotypes was true. Three
months after they brought their son Michael home, they wrote
his birthmother the following letter. Consider how Michael will
benefit when he asks his Mom and Dad, "Where did I come
from?" or "Who are my birthparents?"

To Michael's Birthmother,
Well, where do I begin to tell you how happy
Michael has made us? First let me tell you my name
is Paula and my husband's name is Ken. We would
be happy for you to share your first name with us
if you feel comfortable doing so.
I'll start by telling you a little about Michael.
He weighs about 14 pounds and is about 25 inches
long. He does not have much hair yet so you cannot
really tell what color it is going to be. His eyes were
blue-gray but are gradually turning lighter blue. He
was baptized on March 8. We take him to church

most Sundays. He usually sleeps right through the service, which is sure nice. Even if he is awake, he rarely fusses during the service.

He is a very good baby—he has never cried very much. He is a happy baby—always smiling and "talking." He charms everybody he meets.

He has a bit of a temper when he doesn't get his way. But then, don't we all? He is a very strong baby. He can already creep around when I lay him on his stomach.

Michael has been a very special addition to our family. Since Ken and I cannot have biological children, Michael was a dream come true. Your sacrifice was our gain and we truly appreciate your difficult decision. He is the first grandchild in both families and the first great grandchild on my side of the family. He is loved (and spoiled) by every member of our families.

Now let me try to express our feelings, about you, Michael, and the entire adoption. Please bear with me because I am not very good at writing my feelings down on paper. We really admire you for making the difficult decision that you had to make. You put your own desires aside and thought about what the baby needed. We know this was not an easy thing to do. I will be honest with you and say that had I been in your shoes with this decision to make, I am not sure I could have been as unselfish as you have been. We know that you will never forget Michael and that he will always have a special place in your heart. We hope when you think of him you will be happy because you know he is in a good home with people who love him very much. When I reread that last sentence it occurred to me that you may never really be happy about this decision, but we at least hope you can be at peace with yourself knowing he has loving parents and a good home. I know that the agency has an excellent program for the birth mothers and we are confident that this has helped you handle all the different emotions you must be feeling now.

Sometimes we look at Michael and we have a hard time believing he is really ours. But, because of you he is ours and we can never thank you enough. May God bless you and be with you always.

Paula and Ken

We think Michael's sense of identity can only be strengthened by the love shared between his collective parents.

Adoptive parents benefit in a second powerful way when secrecy disappears. They are able to accept the dignity of their role as adoptive parents. This includes understanding and accepting this role and its realities without feeling second-best to the child's birthparents. There is no subtle message from an influential intermediary that they must fear and compete with the child's "real parents."

The adoptive mother who wrote this next letter has accepted her role as mother to two children who were not born to her. Her role in the life of her children is different from that role either birthmother will have. Different, however, does not mean substitute or second-best. She is simply a mother who loves her children very much:

Dear Birthmother,

I just wanted to let you know how much we are enjoying our new son. We feel so fortunate to have him to love and raise. He has been accepted with joy by all of his new family—grandmas and grandpas, aunts and uncles, and especially by his new dad, mom, and big sister. Our daughter loves to dance and sing for her new brother and to show him off to her friends. And, of course, the baby loves to watch his sister and be with her!

His new dad enjoys talking to our baby about the adventures they will have together when he's old enough to play ball, fish, and hunt! We're all looking forward to camping together this summer.

I thought you'd like to know what a happy and healthy baby our new little one is. He eats well, sleeps well, and loves to "talk" and smile with us. He is such a good baby!

We want you to know that we very much respect the difficult decision you have had to make. You will always have a special place in our hearts for the love that you have felt for our little son. We wish you every happiness in the future. We will make sure that the baby gets the letter you wrote to him when he is old enough to understand. We want him to know how much you cared for him and why he was placed for adoption, and to feel good about himself. We also want him to be happy with his heritage—biological and adoptive—and we try to incorporate traditions which include all of the backgrounds of the people in our very special family. We are happy for our daughter and our new son that they are both adopted. This will be a good thing for them to share. They can help each other to accept the fact that they were adopted. But, please know that we could never love any child any more than we do our two precious children. They are a dream come true for us and always will be.

We wish you health, happiness, and peace.

Sincerely,

Ann

Birthparents also benefit without the imposed secrecy of the second myth. Through the communication opened by the letter exchanges, birthparents learn about the people parenting their child. This information is essential for them to find peace with their adoption decision.

Ralph and Diane, a young married couple, felt unable to parent their first child. They represent the minority of birthparents—those who are married and still choose adoptive placement. It is perhaps harder for society to accept the idea of a married couple placing a child for adoption. So, traditionally, there has been even more of a tendency to place the child veiled in secrecy. Ralph and Diane rejected this mode of placement. While they felt emotionally unprepared for parenthood, they also loved their newborn daughter and had certain specifications for the type of family and environment they wanted for her. In a lengthy letter to the adoptive parents they chose, Ralph and Diane communicated their wishes and their love to their daughter, Jessica, and to her "new" parents. In this fragment from their letter, both pain and generosity come clearly to all of us:

> God really did mean for her to be your baby
> and for you to raise her as your own.

Ralph and Diane will never forget Jessica, but they can take solace in Jessica's growing up an environment and home they chose. Secrecy for this couple, as for most birthparents, would have taken away the social support necessary for their process of grieving. They would have been told to forget rather than encouraged to feel and share their love with their daughter and her adoptive parents.

Shattering the secrecy myth also allows birthparents to feel good about themselves because adoptive parents are consistently supportive of the birthparents, and their letters reflect this encouragement. For the birthparents this opportunity to take pride in their responsible act of adoption is a unique experience. Such encouragement frees birthparents of the guilt and shame so commonly imposed in the past.

Consider how reinforced Colleen must have felt about her decision to place her son, Jed, for adoption after she received the following letter:

> Dear Colleen,
> First, an apology for such a long delay between receiving your letter and Jed's giraffe and this response from us. I'm typing so I can get my thoughts down as fast as they come. We have so very much to share with you! The picture you sent is beautiful, one we will treasure and look forward to sharing with Jed. He favors you in so many features as you will be able to see from the pictures we are enclosing.
> We have truly been blessed with not only a beautiful little boy but such a good baby. He has

been sleeping through the night since Christmas Day! The other night he surprised us by sleeping a long eleven-hour night. The whole family enjoyed that! He has a really happy disposition—loves people and watches everything that goes on around him. When he was just three weeks old we took him to Portland, Maine, for Thanksgiving. It was a long flight and a few plane changes but he fared very well and, even at that young age, watched everything and everyone around. We think he is unusually bright, of course!

At the first visit to the Pediatrician Jed had gained to 10 lbs. and stretched out 1/2 in. He is up to about 12 lbs. now. Since five weeks he has been taking cereal and adding something else new each week. What an eater he is?! Loves bananas (his favorite), squash, applesauce, pears, sweet potatoes (green beans just so-so). We have decided this week that his appetite now parallels the dog's and she is 45 lbs.! He isn't fat but he really is stretching out and growing out of his clothes. (Wears large 3 mos. or small 6 mos. sizes now!)

Jed has been holding his head up strongly since 2 months and follows voices now. Just yesterday Carl watched him turn over for the first time from his tummy to his back and a repeat performance. I was away for the afternoon and missed all the excitement. You must think I am very biased and not sharing anything negative with you. Jed does have a temper but the neat part about it—he usually has a valid complaint and either way he is so easy to console! We both admire that quality in him. No hair! Well, maybe just a little. . . . When the sun shines just right across his "hair" it looks red-blonde to me and his eyelashes are also the same color. He will be a real heart-breaker with his big blue eyes! He has a most charming pug nose (so do I) and a full face that truly lights up when he smiles.

We left Christmas Day to spend the holiday up

North with both of our families. Jed seemed to do pretty well with all the long travel hours, many airports and airplanes and long drives. The relatives just loved him!! Both of our parents felt so much emotion for him and had a hard time letting us take him back home. My parents are looking forward to going to Colorado with us next month and watching Jed during the day while we go skiing. Don't think they have ski sizes to fit Jed—otherwise he would probably want to try it!

Some of Jed's favorite things: watching football games, eating, eating, taking long naps, loves his bath!, getting all dressed up and looking in the mirror, being rocked to sleep, riding in the car listening to soothing music. The list seems to go on and on. . . .

I have shared all I can think of for now, Carl will think of somethings I forgot.

. . . We respect your feelings and want only the things that will help you through this most difficult time in your life. We think of you each day as we look at our beautiful son and we pray for you that the growing that you are doing will be richly blessed. Your decision to carry and nurture Jed so that he could experience life will carry many blessings for you throughout your life. I am convinced of that. Each time I look at him and realize that had someone else conceived him, they may have chosen abortion as an alternate and he would never have been, I thank God he was entrusted to you and now has been brought into our lives.

I look forward to meeting you one day!

With love for you always,
Sandy

The love and gratitude in the above letter release Colleen from any need to live a lifetime feeling guilty about her decision. Colleen, as with many of our birthmothers, has received the social support necessary to parent future children, continue her education, or advance professionally.

Frequently, letters deeply reflect all the sincere gratitude and love felt. Letters also do not simply sing general praises, but become very specific, very personal, and very memorable for the details of human sharing. Here is but one such example:

Dear Parents of My Little Angel,

I deeply appreciate your thoughtfulness and concern for my well-being. I would also like to thank you for sharing with me the joy and happiness you've found in her. One of my main concerns for her was that I wanted her to be well loved by one and all, and you have done just that. I'm also very happy to know that you plan to make her bilingual, since I myself am bilingual. I know of the advantages of being bilingual. Oh, I can go on and on with <u>Thanks</u> to you, for all you have done and will continue to do for her. I can't find the words to express the happiness and relief that I feel. When I first put her for adoption, I thought that I would feel regret for my actions and that she wouldn't be well taken care of. But the more I hear about her wonderful parents, the less I worry about her. And now I'm positive that she will get all that I ever wanted for her.

Thank-you always,
Your daughter's
birth mother

P.S. These earrings, that I want my Little Angel to have, have a special meaning behind them. You see, when I was born, my grandmother went out and bought them for me since I was the first (and only) girl in the family. But since I never got my ears pierced, I wanted her to have them.

I also want her to have this blanket that I crocheted for her. I wanted her to have something that I made. I couldn't decide on what to make at first but once I decided, I got excited and had it made quicker than I expected. Again, <u>Thank-You</u> for wanting my Li'l Angel and for just being You.

The final member in the adoption drama to benefit from the rejection of the second myth is the adoptee. He benefits because his collective parents are permitted to grow secure in their particular roles in his life. His adoptive parents are not unwittingly encouraged to compete to possess him. Nor are his birthparents punished and banished from a place in his life. The adoptee can feel good about the individuals who "together" give him life. He also receives the rare treasure of a personal and truly meaningful letter that he would otherwise be denied.

To My Little Angel,
    A precious, innocent and beautiful child who I have Loved from the moment I was first aware of her presence inside me. I will always Love you, care about you, worry about you and wonder how much you've grown and how your life has turned out to be. My sweet child, you were created out of <u>Love</u>, a love that your biological father and I shared for a couple of years. We were both young, with changes in our own individual lives; changes that were hard for the other to understand and accept, which caused our life together to fall apart. I guess it was time for us to go our separate ways, to be free to experience and be aware of ourselves as individuals. Giving you up for adoption was one of the hardest decisions I ever had to make. I wanted to keep you, to tell everyone that you were mine, to provide everything and more for you and be so very proud. But you see, I had to face the fact that it would have made both of our lives extremely difficult. I wanted you to have the same kind of childhood that I had. Growing up in a family with a set of parents who cared enough to provide the very best of everything. Which was something I could not give you unless I worked at two jobs while I was also trying to continue college. I couldn't see myself leaving you with

someone while I worked day and night with no time for you. Depriving you of the love and attention you so desperately need from a set of full time parents.

So once I decided on adoption, I felt good about my decision and knew it was for the best. We both have a lifetime ahead of us and I know that your parents will make it a happy one for you. I've heard nothing but positive things about them and I couldn't have picked a better set of parents for you myself. As for my life, I will pick up the pieces and make the best of my road to the future.

I've heard people talk against adoption, but they don't see all the aspects and advantages in it. They say that I've lost you forever, but no matter what the circumstances, I see it as "no matter what anyone says, you will always be my child in my heart, only that somewhere on this earth, there is a wonderful couple taking care of you."

Sincerely,

Your birthmother

3
Birthparents
Remember Forever

Myth Number Three:
*"Both the birthmother and birthfather
will forget about their unwanted child."*

The third typical myth endures despite all available information that distinctly proclaims that birthparents remember their birthchild for a lifetime. The most frequent and persuasive source of this information remains the birthparents themselves. As a group, these men and women have circulated expressive and clear statements. Here is an example, from a brochure produced by Concerned United Birthparents, Inc.:

> . . . A birthparent's feelings are not automatically obliterated upon affixing a signature to a contract; however much of society has been led to believe that. Many, perhaps most endure another pain: a "lifelong sense of psychological amputation," wondering if their birthchild is well and happy or even alive! This unique pain defies description.

> Our own experiences support that sensitive CUB statement. No birthmother we have ever known has ever forgotten that little life that was so much a part of her for nine months. Nor have we met a birthfather who easily dismisses the fact he has fathered a child. Mary, an eighteen-year-old birthmother, tells us that after three years she still thinks of her blue-eyed daughter with the love evident in this, her first letter, written seven weeks after her daughter was born:

Dear Daughter,

I've read the social history of your family over and over, and I believe that you will now be able to have the kind of life that I want you to have. Although it was very hard for me to give you up, I feel that it is best for you to have a stable family that will be able to give you all the time and things that you will need.

Your birthfather and I came to Texas from up north. We both love the ocean and being outdoors. I hope that you will have the chance to go to the ocean with your family, and living in the country, I hope you will get to be outside as much as you want.

Your birthfather is a very warm, sensitive person who was with me all through my pregnancy and hospital stay. We care about each other, but we both have a lot of growing and learning to do before we even consider making a lifelong commitment.

When I found out that I was pregnant, many things went through my mind, but I always tried to keep in mind what was best for you. I feel that it is important for you to have a mother and father who not only love you, but are stable in their relationship as well. Our financial condition was another consideration, as it would have been very hard just to buy all the things you would need, and things that you would have wanted would be almost impossible to buy. I also feel that it is important for a family to spend time together, and as I plan on going to college and working, I would not have been able to spend the time with you that I feel is important.

Your birthfather and I love you very much. I hope you will understand that it is because we love you so much that you are now a member of a very special family; ready to give you all the time, attention, love and anything else you may need.

After you were born, I realized how hard it would be to say good-bye to you. You were such a beautiful baby. I could always pick you out in the nursery; you didn't have much hair (that helped me pick you out!), but you were also very special-looking, your eyes were such a <u>beautiful</u> blue, and you were such a good baby. The nurses brought you to me to feed, and each time they brought you, it got harder, and I would cry all over you, and I know that although it was the hardest thing I have ever done, it was the right decision. Your family loves you very much and they will be able to give you all the love, time and special attention that I want you to have.

I always wanted to have a big brother (I have two little brothers) and I hope you will feel lucky to have one.

It's taken me almost seven weeks to write this letter but it's taken me that long to really believe that it was really the right decision. If you ever feel discouraged, always remember that your family wanted you very much, and because we all love you, your birthfather and I, you are now a very special member of a very special family.

All my love,
Your Birthmother

Information disseminated by the Concerned United Birthparent group in the publication "The Birthparent Perspective" also addresses a frequent corollary to the for-getting myth:

> If the birthparents have gone on with their lives and have forgotten, then the social worker, adoption intermediary, and judge must protect their privacy over the adult adoptee's desire to seek a reunion.

This comment and its protective attitude is soundly rejected by most birthparents. Very few want anonymity. Besides which, they rightfully remind powerful individuals in control that they have a right to be asked, before their privacy is automatically protected and their child is denied access to them. As Concerned United Birthparents, Inc., writes in their widely circulated, pamphlet:

Adoptees have the absolute right to full and accurate information about their origins, including identification of, and meeting with, the birthparents, whenever and whatever age there is a need. . . . Our experience—and researchers and activist groups who effect reunions agree—shows that only a scant minority want anonymity. . . . Most birthparents are overjoyed to finally know the fate of their birthchild, and to close a long, painful chapter of wondering.*

Susan, a thirty-four year old birthmother, writes of her long need to someday meet her daughter (whom she had also named Susan). This letter was written fourteen years after her daughter's placement:

Dear Susan,

That's the name I gave you when you were born but I'm sure you're parents have renamed you.

There are so many things that I would like to say to you and so much of my life that I really want to share with you. I'm sure I could never begin to come close in a letter

Until recently I didn't know that it was possible to write you a letter and that you might someday read it and find out that I did love you very much when you were born. I love you very much now and have loved you all these years. Every June on you birthday you are remembered and I say a special prayer for you often.

If you should ever wish to find me, it shouldn't be too hard. Right now I live in San Antonio but won't put the address in here as we are going to be moving to another house soon. We both like San

---

*Concerned United Birthparents, Inc., (Pub.) *The Birthparents' Perspective*, (pamphlet), Milford, MA, (undated).

Antonio and plan to stay here for awhile.

As I said at the beginning of this letter, I want to share so very much with you and I wish you could share all of your life with me. . . . There are so many relatives you could claim I don't know where to start telling you about them. Maybe that would be best left until we meet. Both sets of my grandparents are still living at this time, along with all of my Aunts and Uncles and their children. Not to mention a lot of them on Martin's side of the family.

I am enclosing a picture of Martin and our two children taken last year. They haven't changed too much since then but probably will have by the time you read this. Also enclosed is a picture taken about a year after Martin and I were married. It is from my grandparents 50th wedding anniversary party. It is not too clear but you can get an idea of what everyone looks like. These are my brother and my sisters and myself along with our grandparents—my mother's father and mother.

Well, Susan, I guess you can tell I'm excited about telling you things but I guess I had better close this letter and hope that someday you will want to know more.

If you ever want, need or desire to know me and the rest of your family, we are all here and I am waiting.

You should not take any of this to mean that I ever want to interfere with your life or take any love away from your parents. To me they are very special people and maybe someday they will know from me how much I think of them too.

Only you and they know what it would mean if you try to find me. Don't ever do anything to hurt them because they <u>are</u> your parents.

All my love always,
Your Susan

The myth that birthparents forget persists in spite of clear evidence to the contrary. Such an error is not just the result of folk tales and gossip. This apparent contradiction in logic results very much from the rationalization of adoption intermediaries, families, friends, and adoptive parents. These four powerful influences maintain the myth because of their own need to believe it is true.

For the adoption intermediary to acknowledge that birthparents have lifetime feelings, especially sorrow, about the placement of a child is to recognize the extensive therapy and post-adoption counseling birthparents require. This assistance, of course, consumes time and dollars of the adoption agency and professional intermediary. How much easier to rationalize away the aftermath of adoption, rather than to develop a program to treat the effects of a "psychological amputation." Therefore, the intermediary tends to cling to the belief that the birthparents quickly dismiss their adoption experience and their child. Only this belief permits the professional guilt-free termination of contact after the birth of the child and after the relinquishment papers are signed.

For the family member of a birthparent, loss of a child through adoption compares to the loss of a child through death. Interestingly, while family members are assisted in their grief over the death of a family member, rarely does society condone the same grief when a family member is lost because of an adoptive placement. Yet, for some, the placement of a child might mean the loss of a grandchild they will never know.

The following letter was written to Marsha's birthson whom she placed for adoption at one week. Marsha speaks of the involvement of her birthson's grandmother. Although her letter does not indicate this, Marsha's mother said goodbye to her first and only grandchild in the few minutes she held him close:

> Dear Son,
>
> First of all I want you to know that I love you very much and I always will. I'm writing this letter to let you know why I put you up for adoption. It wasn't an easy decision but I was thinking of you and your life. I wanted you to have the best life possible. I was in a position where I couldn't make

that happen. Let me explain the situation between your father and I. We didn't know each other very long before I became pregnant. But we did care for each other very much. We were both young and we weren't ready to raise a baby the way it should be done. Your father didn't earn enough money for all three of us much less himself. We didn't want you to have a hard time growing up. We wanted you to be happy. I hope you can understand that I was only thinking of what was best for you.

I didn't want to give you up but I did it out of love for you. I really wish it had been different and I'm sorry it wasn't.

I thought it would be nice if you knew a little about your grandparents. When I was pregnant with you they made sure I took good care of myself and you. Your grandmother especially made sure I took care so that you would come out to be the beautiful and healthy little baby you were. They wanted you to have a good home and be happy too. When we were in the hospital they came to visit everyday. That first time I saw you was a very special day. When I got to hold you for the first time you were sleeping peacefully in my arms. I didn't want to let you go. I wanted to hold you forever. I will never forget that day. Your grandmother held you next. She looked so happy and said you were a beautiful baby. You hardly cried at all, you were a good baby. You had a beautiful smile. I even got to feed you and that also was a special time for me. You ate so well that I knew you were going to grow up strong and healthy.

I thought I would let you know that I had a name for you. It's Mitchell. I will always treasure those moments I had with you. I hope that where ever you are, you're happy. I will always be wondering where you are and what you're doing. Please take care son. I love you so very much.

Love Always,
Your Birthmother

Grandparents like Marsha's mother do miss their grand-child. Their mourning, however, is done in silence. They too want to believe their own children forget because that frees them from dwelling on their own pain and possible guilt at their inability to do more to prevent "their own loss."

For other family members the need to believe that the birthparents forget is the easiest way to deny the experience. Peggy's father would not deal with his sixteen-year-old's unwed pregnancy. When Peggy wrote her birthson the fol-lowing letter, both her pain and her family's pain was made obvious. Peggy's father will continue to believe that both Peggy and her mother will forget because he desperately wants the painful topic to be honorably closed:

Dear Son,

I am writing this letter to you in hope that you may understand why I had to have you adopted.

I am 19 years old and the only daughter of four. I have one brother older than I and two younger than I. My father has always thought of me as his little girl. I guess he always will.

I was sixteen when I became pregnant with you. Both my parents were hurt. Since I don't believe in abortion, I decided to go ahead and have you. I wanted to keep you so very much.

But not being married, my father thought it best I have you adopted. It broke my heart to have to give you away. My mother wanted you as much as I did, but my father insisted. My father is very old fashioned and is set in his ways, so my preg-nancy was very wrong to him. You see, I had to have you adopted. There was no way my father would let me keep you.

I must go now. Remember that I will love you always and will always hold a place in my heart for you. Please be happy and have a wonderful life.

All My Love,
Your Birthmother

Friends of birthparents are motivated to believe the third

myth by their own feelings of compassion and a sense of inadequacy. Assisting a birthparent through the adoption experience requires tremendous knowledge and understanding of the dynamics of fear, guilt, and sorrow. Ill-prepared to handle the situation, especially the aftermath of the placement, friends often evade the subject. Not wanting to awaken their friend's anguish, they avoid the topic through rationalizing, "Carol and Jay have forgotten so don't remind them by talking about it."

Finally, adoptive parents seek the comfort of the third myth. Most adoptive parents (or their family members and friends) know stories of birthmothers who changed their minds and sought to regain custody. Therefore, many adoptive parents instinctively react to calm their fear of this scenario by denying the possibility that their child's birthparents could have a continued emotional bond to the child. They believe birthparents go away and forget because they want to believe that. As one adoptive father confirmed, "When I acknowledge that Jamie's birthmother still cares for him then I open up all the old scares that she might want him back."

Although we fully appreciate the powerful needs of others to maintain the myth that birthparents forget, we reject such an unfair and disproportionate burden being placed upon the birthparents. Perpetuating this myth prolongs the stereotype of uncaring and unfeeling baby makers (remember the first myth). Most importantly, the third myth denies birthparents post adoption counseling from the adoption professional and emotional support from family and friends. This, in effect, abandons two people at a time when assistance is most needed during their natural mourning period. Without social support, birthparents are handicapped in their ability to resolve their decision and to constructively rebuild their lives.

We firmly reject the temptation by many adoption intermediaries to provide little or no post adoption counseling because of their belief in this myth. We have structured counseling and support groups to assist our birthparents. We also strive to help family members and friends of our birthparents by involving them in the therapy routinely provided after the child's adoption. Our objective is to help these individuals clarify and directly face the emotions that cause them to seek the solace of the third myth. When they no longer need to deny that birthparents spend a lifetime remembering their child, family members and friends can help the birthparents and themselves deal with a myriad of feelings.

A sister of one of our birthmothers wrote the following letter to the adoptive parents of her niece. She no longer has a need to rationalize away the depth of feelings awakened for herself and for her sister by the placement of "their" child. Neither woman will ever forget:

Dear Special Parents,

I'm really not sure how to start this letter. I am the birthmother's sister. I'm a year older than her, graduated from high school this year and plan to go to college in the future.

When I read the letter you wrote my sister, I felt so much joy that words couldn't express my feelings. We were all so happy to hear about the baby that, at that moment, the letter meant more to all of us than anything in the world. I know it was very hard for my sister to give her baby up, but I feel she did the best for the baby.

You both seem like such wonderful parents that it's like you were a gift from God.

I'm so overwhelmed that the baby was so lucky as to have such parents that I know will give her all the love that is humanly possible.

There were many nights that I cried myself to sleep hoping and praying that the baby would become a very special part of her adoptive parents' heart as she has for us.

I hope that you will continue to write my sister on how the baby is progressing.

If I'm not asking too much, could you give the baby a kiss and a hug for me? It would mean so much to me.

Thank you both for being such perfect parents. May God be with you all and protect you always.

Sincerely,
A thankful birthmother's sister

Besides working with the family members and friends of birthparents to counter the third myth, we counsel our adoptive parents to acknowledge and deal with their feelings toward birthparents. Frequently, adoptive parents harbor the notion that birthparents have a natural right to withdraw their consent to an adoption. It is commonly believed that birthparents can and often do successfully reclaim their children. Let us compare this belief to the legal realities.

Adoption in the United States is purely statutory in nature. Each state establishes its own regulations in this matter. As a general rule there must be strict compliance with the applicable state law in order to place a minor child into an adoptive family. Birthparents must voluntarily consent to the adoptive placement of their child and this is usually accomplished by executing with full understanding a formal surrender document.

Generally, birthparents have *no absolute right* to revoke their consent if their surrender was freely and voluntarily given. Moreover, under various adoption statutes, approval of the court is essential to withdrawal of a birthparent's consent. These laws give the court discretionary power to allow or refuse the request for withdrawal. The court exercises this discretion in the best interest of the child and in accordance with the reasonableness of each birthparent's claim.

A birthparent who does seek to withdraw a previously granted consent to adoption must show that good cause exists to set aside such consent. An attempted withdrawal based on whim or caprice or motivated solely by a change of heart or mind will not result in the consent being revoked. The birthparent has the burden to prove that the consent was procured by such circumstances as fraud, duress, undue influence, or overreaching. In actuality this burden is not frequently met, but if a birthparent does prove that consent was not freely executed, the court will allow the consent to be revoked. The very few such cases seem to receive disproportionate television and newspaper coverage, adding to the social perception that birthparents often withdraw their consent to an adoption. In total, although the fear of possibly losing the adoptee is very real to many adoptive parents, the legal reality is that revocation of properly executed surrenders happens much more frequently on soap operas than in real life.

Directly facing and discussing the fear of legally or emotionally losing the adoptee is a powerful start for the adoptive parent toward gaining insight. We appreciate the fact that only adoptive parents deal with the sometimes crippling thought that if the birthparents do change their minds, they as adoptive parents might lose a court battle. Uniqueness, however, does not make the adoptive parents' fears unmanageable or even unparalleled to other life experiences.

All parents routinely deal with fears surrounding the safety of their children. For example, parents do not hesitate to admit they worry that their child will be injured in a car wreck, and that motivates them to use seat belts. The same parents neither dwell on that apprehension nor deny its existence. Instead they simply accept it. We strive for our adoptive parents to have a similar acceptance of their fear of their child being reclaimed. We firmly believe that adoptive parents should not deny or dwell on anxieties that might tempt them to believe birthparents go away and forget, nor should adoptive parents expect their fears to totally disappear.

Recently, one of our adoptive couples felt secure enough to have a face-to-face meeting with the birthmother of their second son. Yet, they admitted to the fleeting thought, "We momentarily visualized her coming into the room with a gun to kidnap Chris." This couple can speak rationally of their momentary fantasy, but the fact is that they were still insecure even as they prepared to meet the young birthmother. Their fear may never totally disappear, and that is okay. The real positive for this couple is their ability to tell us and others about their experience without letting a soap-opera type fear dictate their decisions about their lives.

Once again, our experiences with the letter exchanges have been positive in relation to the third myth of adoption. Adoptive parents working with us learn firsthand that birthparents do not forget. Letters also teach adoptive parents to accept their fears of reclaiming without seeking the solace of the third myth.

Lisa, an eighteen-year-old birthmother, wrote the following letter describing her continued love for her birthdaughter one year after placement:

Dear adoptive family,

I can't tell you how much your letter and picture at Christmas meant to me. I guess the hardest thing for me to deal with was giving my little girl to strangers. It really made me feel good to hear from you. I know sharing your feelings with me wasn't easy, but I feel so much more comfortable knowing a little bit about you.

As her first birthday approaches I think about you often. I pray for you and hope that all is well. I don't want you to feel pressured, but if you feel comfortable writing, I am open to hear from you again.

The birthfather and I are still together. He shares in wishing you all the best. He is working as a carpenter, and really likes his work. I am working as a night auditor, and am trying to get some college credit as well. I keep pretty busy.

Please give your daughter an extra birthday hug and kiss from her birthmother and birthfather.

With best wishes and all our love,
Birthmother & Birthfather

The recipients of this letter might have been frightened by Lisa's obvious love for her birthchild and request for future information. Certainly, the time had passed for the myth to have worked its magic and made Lisa forget her little girl. The adoptive parents, however, were not frightened. They took great comfort in learning about Lisa and about the birthfather of their daughter. Of course, these adoptive parents did not miss Lisa's reference to "your daughter," but that particular assurance is not as necessary as it once might have been. Their fears are no longer unmanageable.

Our letter exchanges have also clearly communicated that although birthparents may be sad or depressed at times, these feelings do not mean they would change their decision. Most birthparents feel like Debbie, who wrote three years after placement:

I placed Craig for adoption so there would be as few disruptions in his life as possible. So my coming back to take him from his family would defeat my whole purpose.

Another birthparent, Valerie, expresses similar reassurance in her letter to the adoptive parents of her daughter. Valerie affirms them as parents, while still being interested in her child's development:

Dear Sharon and Steve,
    Yes, it has been a while since we have had contact, but now is a good time to say "hello" again. I am sure everything is going beautifully with the family and with our prayers it will stay that way always.
    As time goes by, I keep thinking about that little angel ya'll have and how happy she must be. Surely she is growing prettier every minute. But she isn't a baby anymore, she's a little girl. She walks and talks and knows everyone's name. Soon she'll learn colors, numbers, and letters with the help of her smart parents and swell surroundings. But all I can remember is her as a tiny baby like the day she was born. I can't _even_ imagine her standing up (that's how long it's been)!!! I would like to fill my imaginations of a little girl instead of a baby very badly, but I think I need some help.
    Can you please send me a short letter and tell me how that little angel is doing? I would be so happy it would make me cry with joy! It would be an early Christmas present for me and my parents. We would be ever so grateful. If it's not asking too much may we also get a picture of her! It would be nice to picture her as a little girl in my mind when I pray for her.
    Thank you.
                        Always,
                        Valerie

The adoptive parents who received this letter will no longer perpetuate the myth that birthparents forget their birthchild. They know Valerie will never forget her daughter, but that fact is no longer alarming.

Other birthmothers share through their letters how they respect both the adoptive parents of their child and the integrity of that parent-child relationship. Kim, for example, addressed her letter to "My Baby's Parents:"

To My Baby's Parents,

It's so hard for me to begin this letter, so much I would like you to understand that giving my son up for adoption was the hardest decision I ever had to make. I am just so glad I was able to do it. No mother likes to think her child would be better off without her. But, I realize that isn't true. I couldn't give my son everything I wanted him to have. And I wanted him to have the world. But you could. You were able to give him everything I wanted for him. But what makes it even nicer was knowing that you were doing everything because you love him too! Not because you had to, but because you wanted to. I know that bringing children up today is challenging and involved. I realize you have your work cut out for you. But I know everything will work out fine. I believe in your new family.

I don't regret any decision I have made concerning my baby. It was hard letting him go. I know it was in his best interest. I did it because I love him and cared only about his interest, his life. I will never forget my son, I never want to forget. He will always remain a part of me. My love always with him.

I realize he's your son now. We all have played such a vital part in his beginning. I gave him life and then I gave him to you. You will shape that life and make him into a fine young man. I am so glad he has you. I am so glad you're there for him. I couldn't have found two better people to be his parents if I had done the choosing myself.

After he was born, I started believing that God does work in mysterious ways. He gave me the son

I had always dreamed of. Then He made it possible for me to give my baby a family. Something I wanted so much for him to have. And He gave you the child you wanted so much.

I'd like to think God planned this from the very beginning. I believe on September 23 I not only gave birth to a beautiful baby boy, I gave birth to a start of a family.

I will never be able to thank you enough for everything, for just being there when I need you, when my son needed you. I know that he's happy and loved now with you both. I could not have asked for anything more. I hope and pray your home and lives are filled with nothing but love and laughter. Thank you so much. I feel nothing but love and good wishes for you both and your family.

Gratefully and Sincerely Yours,

Kim

Kim speaks of her love for the parents of her birthson and the love was warmly received by Ron and Kathy. As adoptive parents, Ron and Kathy might at times need to deal with a recurrence of the thought that Kim will change her mind. Both, however, have learned to calmly accept this as part of parenthood.

The open communication and trust that can develop through the letter exchanges constitute a productive rejection of the third myth. The human tendency to believe and maintain a"forgetting" fiction is replaced by a healthy desire to know and to assist both birthparents. Most importantly, as adoptees hear about their birthparents, they will have the opportunity to learn accurate stories of continued love.

4
A Search For Roots, Not Different Parents

Myth Number Four:
*"If the adoptee really loved his adoptive
family, he would not have to search
for his birthparents."*

Curiosity and interest in one's past or future lineage speaks well of a healthy, inquisitive mind. The enthusiasm which greeted Alex Haley's *Roots* indicates that modern American society wholeheartedly endorses inquiring into one's heritage—unless you are an adoptee For adoptees, yearning to know about their heritage is still disapprovingly labeled an ungrateful act.

The basis of the fourth myth of adoption—that curbs the adoptee's hunger to know his heritage—stems from a misguided desire to reward adoptive parents for their unselfish act of adopting. The myth's professed objective is to spare the two individuals who willingly labored to parent "someone else's child"—spare them the hurt of rejection from the child seeking his "real parents." The myth actually sets up scenarios of the present family unit being dismantled in favor of a new family. The most common picture is the ungrateful adoptee who abandons his adoptive parents to love his "natural mother."

The fourth myth is also designed to punish birthparents for an unwed parenthood. This time the objective is to discipline the individuals who conceived a child but dared not to parent him. Society mandates a righteous punitive measure for such a "sin"—lifetime separation.

Tragically, the adoptee's welfare is ignored in both the rewarding and punishing aspects of the fourth myth. Adoptees are the only individuals in the United States denied knowledge of their genealogy. By the laws of most states, they are not allowed access to their original birth certificates, nor to the court records and adoption agency files of their adoption. These documents alone contain the identity of their birthparents and the social and medical histories that many adoptees seek to orient themselves in their own existence.

Through our post-adoption work, we daily encounter adoptees seeking accurate information about their origins and their genetic potential. Contrary to what advocates of the myth would have us believe, these are not unhappy adoptees running away from home and their nonunderstanding parents. These are adoptees who talk easily about contented childhoods and close family relationships. Yet they recount numerous unanswered questions about their biological identity. They report recurrent dreams about their "abandonment." They even have distorted fantasies and daydreams about their birthparents.

They have two universal questions: The simple one which non-adoptees would take for granted, "Who do I look like?" and then the loaded question that seeks confirmation of self-worth, "Why was I given away?" We have learned from these adoptees that the identity crisis of adolescence impacts the adoptee in unique ways. One adoptee recalled those turbulent years:

> I needed to know who I was, and what I was all about. But I had no way to find out.

Another adoptee, now twenty years old, related how she "set out" as a teenager to get pregnant and keep her baby. "I wanted a child because I desperately needed a bloodline. I needed to actually touch someone related to me."

Marriage and pregnancy can also frighten the adoptee. Some adoptees fear a possible incestuous marriage to a blood relative. Other adoptees, denied information about their genetic make up, worry about what kind of child they will conceive. "Will I pass on a crippling disease?" they wonder.

The search for a medical history is itself a need to be complete. Kelly, age thirty-two, recalls always being traumatized when going to a new doctor. Every new doctor would ask about her medical history and when she revealed that she was adopted, he would simply tear the medical history form in two. Each time she was humiliated by such an overt reminder of the void in her background.

We have also observed how subsequent parenthood for the adoptee is usually a time of extreme joy. They finally know a "blood relative!" Adult adoptees, in fact, express an almost childlike delight in at last knowing someone who looks like them.

In sum, adoptees are not running away from their adoptive parents. Nor do they want to intrude in the birthparents' lives. They simply seek background information to untangle their pasts and help predict their future.

We reject the practice of the adoptee being blocked from his roots by restrictive laws and the social attitudes propagating the fourth myth. Betty Jean Lifton, a writer, experienced the terrible aloneness of being an adopted adult denied access to her genetic background. We share Ms. Lifton's belief that adoptees need a sense of continuity and belonging that may only come through their search for origins. Ms. Lifton wrote, in 1979:

> The struggle for a sense of identity is common to all of us. For an adoptee it takes on an uncommon dimension. Cut off from blood roots, the adoptee is often deeply troubled by feelings of abandonment and alienation. There is a sense of nonexistence, of never having been born.*

Unfortunately, today's adult adoptee has grown up in a society which still believes in the fourth myth. He has been conditioned to believe that he would be "ungrateful" to his adoptive parents if he searched. Thirsty for simple pieces of

---

*Lifton, Betty Jean, *Lost & Found: The Adoption Experience,* New York, N Y, The Dial Press, 1979.

information but guilty about possibly hurting Mom and Dad, the adoptee is caught in an emotional tug-of-war. He must possess great strength and determination to actually pursue his search, and even then the actual process of searching is often frustrating and painful.

Regrettably, the adoption agency (which is generally one of the first places the adoptee goes for information) also subscribes to the fourth myth. The agency can be negative and punitive to the adoptee saying "Why do you want to search; aren't you happy with your adoptive parents?" or "You should be grateful—just think how much this will hurt your adoptive parents."

The adoptee is further blocked in his search by his own fears. Since he too has grown up with the messages of myth number one ("Your birthmother obviously doesn't care about you or she wouldn't have given you away") and number three ("Both your birthmother and birthfather have forgotten you"), the adoptee fears rejection by his birthparents. He most dreads an uncaring birthmother rejecting him a second time!

Again the adoption agency and professional intermediary support the myths by warning the adoptee that his birthmother wants confidentiality:

What about your birthmother's rights—what if she doesn't want to be found?

The intermediary might even imply, with a kind of calculating cliché, that the adoptee will find something negative if he pursues his search.

One's roots and origins, no matter how apparently sordid in the eyes of middle-class laymen and professionals, are a part of a person's reality. Circumstances under which a birthparent relinquished a birthchild are invariably understandable if the facts and full truth of their life situation are known. Rarely, if ever, do birthparents give up that role without great reluctance and cost to themselves. Most often the welfare of their child is their main concern. To deny the adoptee access to these facts is to lock the adoptee into negative fantasizing about his birthparents and ultimately about himself.

Fear of the unknown can cripple any one of us in our

search for personal growth; therefore, we hope adoption intermediaries and society in general will be able to free themselves from the fourth myth. The stress and negativism imposed by the mandate not to search should be lifted from the adult adoptee. He may have simple curiosity or a specific need to know his origins and genetic potential. We think that he, like any other adult, deserves that freedom of choice.

We also reject the fourth myth's attempt to protect "unselfish" adoptive parents. We admit that on first reflection, there is something threatening to a parent about a child wanting to go off and find his or her "real parents." It feels like a rejection, as if the adoptive parents were not all they should have been; but when examined from the perspective of the adoptee's need, good parenting involves encouraging the adoptee's curiosity and preparing him for all of life's independent searches.

Our experiences with adoptees convince us that the search for origins does not result in the adoptive parents losing their son or daughter. Adoptive parents and society must understand the role the adoptee's collective parents maintain—his birthparents gave him the reality of birth and heritage, and his adoptive parents give him the reality of parenting and nurturing. One cannot take the other's place. Each parent is real in a unique way; no parent is better or worse. The adoptee has a connection to all his parents which is as real as his life, given or nurtured.

Kelly, the adoptee we referred to earlier who was haunted by her lack of a medical history, did hunt for her answers. What she found was, first, a birthmother who could answer her questions about her medical background, and second, a sensitive person who—wondrously—looks like her. (She had always wondered where she got her "ethnic" nose.) In addition, Kelly found a friend to share numerous identical interests. Today, Kelly maintains ongoing contact with her birthmother. She described their relationship as two good friends, and like good friends they correspond and visit with each other regularly.

Kelly is quick to add she still considers her adoptive parents as her parents. That relationship is solidly built on a foundation of shared memories, mutual respect, and tender love. Her adoptive parents' nurturing and continued presence are as essential to Kelly today as was their support when she first braved a pursuit for answers. The fact that Kelly has ongoing contact with her birthmother does not signify that her adoptive parents have lost. Kelly's bond to her adoptive parents is not so fragile that the ties could be erased or weakened simply because Kelly likes or even learns to love the woman who gave her life.

Unfortunately, many adoptees who search for their origins do not share their pursuit with their adoptive parents. They fear that their parents will be hurt, so out of loyalty and love they do not talk of their need to know. It is especially sad to hear Dick, a twenty-seven-year-old adoptee, tell a room full of adoptive parents how his exploration for and actual meeting with his birthmother reaffirmed his admiration and tenderness for his adoptive parents. Yet his adoptive parents cannot share this knowledge. Dick has never been able to tell them he was "ungrateful" enough to search for and find his birthmother, so he cannot now share his stronger love for them.

Some adoptees locked in by loyalty and the myth choose to wait to conduct their search until after their adoptive parents die. This ability to set aside one's own needs in order to protect a loved one from possible pain reflects their deep love and loyalty. Amy, for example, is a twenty-year-old adoptee who has a great desire to look for her birthparents but she also refuses to hurt her adoptive parents. She thinks her search would hurt them because they have never been able to talk about her birthmother without tears in their eyes. Amy has chosen to postpone any inquiry until after her parents' deaths. Since her adoptive parents are older than her birthparents, Amy is willing to risk that her birthparents will still be alive at that time.

Unfortunately, the fourth myth has prevented Dick and Amy from openly and honestly talking to their adoptive parents. Dick's and Amy's parents will be forever denied the opportunity to fully appreciate the depth of their children's love. Additionally, these parents are robbed of an opportunity to grow. They will never learn that just as parents can love more than one child, so too can an adoptee, like Dick or Amy, love more than one mother or one father.

The issue is not which set of parents has the greater right, nor which set the adoptee will love the most. A loved child will mature into a loving adult who will not waste that love, but who may share that love in many different ways. Adoptees frequently tell us that seeking and finding their birthparents does not lessen their love for their adoptive parents (who remain Mom and Dad). Permission to know one's heritage only makes the adoptee love his adoptive parents more—for giving him freedom and for trusting his love.

We also firmly refuse to accept the punishment aspect of the fourth myth, reserved for "sinful" birthmothers. Adoption laws often block birthparents, even more than adult adoptees, from searching and finding. If a birthparent ventures to search, too often curiosity is hatefully labeled "unnatural" by busy intermediaries and conservative judges. Remember, the third typical myth would have a birthparent believe, "You should have forgotten by now."

We support the birthparents' desire and perogative to someday know their child. We find their curiosity to be a healthy reflection of their caring for their birthchild. In addition, such curiosity is reassuring for the adoptee afraid to be twice rejected, afraid to start his own search.

Russell, a nineteen-year-old birthfather, relates his need to someday meet his daughter in a personal letter to her. His love clearly deserves no punishment:

> Dear Daughter,
>
> I want to start this letter by telling you how sorry I am, although I am not sorry for placing you for adoption, I am only sorry that we cannot spend our lives together. Although I only really knew you for a day, I will miss you, and I will always have you in my heart.
>
> The situation between your birthmother and me was that we both loved you very much, but we didn't love each other. We could give you love but not a home. A child needs a home with two people who care and love that child together. This your birthmother and I could not provide, and it is this that I am sorry for. Our decision was a difficult one,

because it is not easy to give up one so dear. The only way we could do this was because we knew through adoption you would get the chance you really deserve to grow up healthy and happy. I pray that you will forgive us and understand why we placed you for adoption.

By the time you read this letter you will have grown enough to hopefully know why we did what we did. Your birthmother and I love you very much. I hope this letter will help you as much as it has helped me. I shall never forget you, and I will always have the hope that someday we will meet, so that we can satisfy both our curiosity, and see what each other is really like. Daughter, have a wonderful life, and I Love You.

> Love Always,
> Your Birthfather
> Russell

We reject a myth that would punish Russell or any birthparent who feels, "We could give you love but not a home." Concerned United Birthparents (CUB) probably sums the birthparent's right and need for information most dramatically in the following statement:

To never know your birthchild is to spend a lifetime in anguish of forever wondering, a punishment disproportionate to the crime of giving birth and allowing another to parent the child.*

We work to counter the fourth myth by first exploring with our adoptive parents the dynamics of the adoptee's need to search. An adoptee's curiosity and fundamental quest for roots is shared by everyone. For the adoptee, however, two "other" parents exist somewhere. This fact alone converts the quest for roots from an intellectual pursuit to a dramatic life experience. Their search is to find a sense of continuity, to

---

* Campbell, Lee H. (Editor), *Understanding the Birthparent*, Milford, MA, Concerned United Birthparents, Inc, 1978.

avoid the grief of permanent separation and loss, and to learn a biological identity.

Once we explore the adoptee's need to search for his or her answers, we assist our adoptive parents to examine the unsettling fears triggered by this reality. Do they still believe their child would not search if he loved them enough? As with all fears, we encourage our adoptive parents to acknowledge and experience them, not deny them.

Fears that they will lose their child to his "real parents" or even that their child will find out "bad things" about his birth-parents are unique to adoptive parents. But these fears can be managed. Understanding the adoptee's need to search does help the adoptive parent. Most frequently we see our parents transforming the hurt of the fourth myth to the awareness and sensitivity displayed in the following letter:

> Dear Birthmother of my Daughter,
>
> I've been wanting to write you but I am sure you realize finding the words to express my feelings is difficult. Sunday in church the thoughts of you ran through my mind as I was again reminded of God's love that he gave his only Son for me. I compared your gift of love to His. It's a gift of love that is a continuing gift of love, love that grows daily. It's a gift of love that I'm sure was a great price for the giver and for that we are more grateful than we can possibly express.
>
> Getting this baby was a long and painful process for us. I'll spare you the details but I want you to know how deeply wanted this child is and therefore, how special. The joy when we first saw her was a high that I've never experienced. It was love at first sight for both of us ....
>
> I have some hopes for your future, too. I hope your future brings the realization of your goals. Your continuing welfare will always be in my prayers. I'm sure you would like to close off this episode of your life although I don't mean forgetting. I'm sure you never will but I want to leave you with the confidence that our daughter is in a home

where she is truly wanted and where she will grow up surrounded by love. I also want you to know that when she learns about you, I will do my best to convey to her that it was your love for her that has given us the chance to grow as a loving family and that she can love you and be grateful to you also.

Now for something painful I feel is necessary to tell you. Someday our daughter may want to find you. I will do my best to bring her up confident of her being loved and respecting your right to your life which does not need to reopen old wounds. I want her to respect that right of yours, however, if when she is grown she feels it is necessary to find you I will not try to prevent her doing so and will even help. I'm sure you must have considered this possibility and I felt compelled to tell you how I feel about it. Should you choose to respond to my letter you may want to say something about your feelings on this matter that I would be able to share with our daughter to help her understand.

I'm having difficulty in finding words to close this letter. I want you to know something of the fantastic enjoyment and pleasure I am experiencing in the daily care of my happy, healthy, growing daughter and her father's deep pride and loving care. We wish you joy, love and peace in your life and from the bottom of our hearts we thank you for the joy, love and peace you have given us.

Your daughter's
Mother and Father

As the preceding letter indicates, adoptive parents working with us no longer regard an adoptee's need to search as a negative statement about their ability to parent. Nor do they believe the myth's prediction of an inevitable loss. One assertive mother soundly rejected the fourth myth and the people who believe it when she commented,

It only hurts if adoptive parents can't separate

themselves from their child's need for a biological identity.

As this adoptive mother understands, effective adoptive parenting involves the realization that adoptees search for their origins, not for replacement parents.

Once adoptive parents deal with their own fears, they, too, seek out the birthparents who can supply the missing answers. Adoptive parents want accurate data about their child's biological family history. Our experience shows that adoptees who grow up having "I don't know" as answers to their questions begin to distrust the adoptive parents. "What are they hiding from me and why?" they frequently question. Therefore, no secrecy can be allowed here because our adoptive parents want information the adoptee can trust.

Through our letter exchanges adoptive parents are rarely forced to say, "I don't know." They have a ready and open communication channel to the persons best able to answer. The family structure is not inadvertently weakened by unanswerable questions. The adoptee, in fact, is supported in his pursuit for origins and a whole identity by his collective parents.

Actually openness and ongoing communication between all members of the adoption drama nullify the need for a myth designed to protect and punish. Adoptive parents need no protection from a loss or hurt that will never occur. Caring birthparents deserve no punishment for their act of creating life.

Janet and Ray are adoptive parents who want to develop a trusting and strong family bond with their new daughter, Ann. They no longer harbor the fourth myth so they both feel that it is natural for intimate members of the adoption drama to want to reach out and know each other. They wrote Ann's birthmother the following letter the night before they brought Ann home:

> It is the night before we see our new adopted daughter for the first time. There is absolutely no way on earth that we can express to you all the joy that we feel. Tomorrow, without a doubt, is one of

the happiest days of our lives!

In all of our joy our thoughts are with you. The adoption agency had given us more of an insight as to how you must feel. We imagine the decision you made to give her up was the most difficult one you've made in your life. We wish there was a way to alleviate your sorrow. We hope, however, you may find some comfort in sharing our joy and in knowing that we so deeply love this little girl even though we haven't seen her. We plan to tell her all about you; how kind, gentle, and unselfish you must be to forsake your own happiness for hers.

We thank you, kind lady, for the joy you have brought to us and vow to treasure and love the precious gift you have bestowed upon us. May you find only happiness and God Bless You!

Janet and Ray, as do our other adoptive parents, reject the fourth myth's mandate of no searching. Ann will be raised with all the knowledge her collective parents can provide. In addition, Ann will not be told the "chosen child" story that reflects society's biased fourth myth—"a child specially chosen and given sufficient love by adoptive parents will not want to know her heritage."

Our children were born to real persons, not magically chosen from a crib in an agency, somewhere, one day. They each have a birthmother and a birthfather who care and who will not forget. They have heritages and genetic potentials that they can claim. As nurturing parents and concerned professionals, we must do everything we can to help our adoptees to grow up healthy and whole. That includes helping them find any missing pieces of their own precious identities.

Part Two:
Beyond The Myths

To this point our book has focused on the four most pervasive myths of adoption:

1. The birthmother obviously doesn't care about her child or she wouldn't have given him away.

2. Secrecy in every phase of the adoption process is necessary to protect all parties.

3. Both the birthmother and birthfather will forget about their unwanted child.

4. If the adoptee really loved his adoptive family, he would not have to search for his birthparents.

These statements represent the prevalent myths in today's adoption drama. We began our book with these myths in order to firmly set in our reader's mind the present image of adoption. Sadly, the four myths are accepted to some extent by everyone. Effects of the myths go beyond outdated agency policies as they permeate interactions between each adult and child touched by adoption.

The following chapters are aimed at making adoption today as myth-free as possible. As we introduce concepts of adoption counseling, pregnancy counseling, and open communication, readers must evaluate how they feel about our practices. If you feel uneasy about a particular idea, check which myth you still (perhaps unconsciously) believe. Our concepts are tested daily—even hour by hour—in human exchanges and interactions we will share. If we are all fortunate, adoption will grow beyond the myths.

5
The Vulnerability
Of Adoptive Parents

"My infertility resides in my heart as an old friend. I do not hear from it for weeks at a time, and then, a moment, a thought, a baby announcement or some such thing, and I will feel the tug—maybe even be sad or shed a few tears. And I think, 'There's my old friend.' It will always be part of me. . . ."
　　　　　Barbara Eck Menning
　　　　　Infertility: A Guide for the
　　　　　Childless Couple (1977)

Typically the "American Dream" consists of the following ingredients: growing up, obtaining a usable education that leads to a comfortable job, getting married, and easily producing children. An alternate ingredient of adopting children is not contemplated since the ability to bear children is always viewed as a "given." In this chapter, we deal with people and their feelings when denied this given. We will introduce the reader to the special type of pain the infertility experience awakens, then explore how a couple's infertility crisis shapes their initial approach to an adopted child.

Finally we will focus on the reality of the adoptive family structure and the struggle to accept that reality.

A STRUGGLE TO ACCEPT INFERTILITY

We are indoctrinated early in life to dream of someday having
children like ourselves. Most couples assume this will automatically happen when they are ready to have children. A
couple's first reaction to the shock of not conceiving is to try
harder. This, in turn, begins a period where the need to get
pregnant seems to overshadow everything else. Many couples tell us of the frustration and tension that develop in their
sexual relationship. They feel required to perform at a specific, clinically determined time. Love and spontaneity are
removed from their sexual relationship. Instead, everything is
focused on their one goal in life—to achieve a pregnancy.

Sadness and defeat grow as the couple struggles with
the often long and painful interval of infertility tests, unsuccessful medical and surgical treatments, and possibly mis-
carriages. Our experience has been that the crisis of infertility
impacts women more profoundly than their spouses. This is
partially explained by the inability of the woman to experience
the physical changes of pregnancy. Frequently, women relate
to us tearful episodes upon learning of a friend's pregnancy.
Gloria was so obsessed with her own inability to conceive that
she was even unable to visit her best friend when that friend
gave birth to her first child. Gloria could not face the reality of
anyone else having a baby—the baby she was being denied.

Other couples caught by the agony of infertility imagine
what it would be like to have a baby. They picture the Lamaze
classes, being in the delivery room, the joy of seeing their
baby born, and the look on their own father's face when
he first sees his grandson or granddaughter. Fantasies such
as these are common because they allow a temporary
escape for the couple desperate to undo the nightmare of
their childlessness.

Society unknowingly adds to the struggle by depicting in
articles and television commercials what is "right" for a person of a certain age and marital status. Friends and family
members ask innocent yet painful questions that presuppose

the couple's ability to have babies. Parents are famous for regularly asking about when they will become grandparents. Their questions pointedly assume that the couple is "selfishly" choosing to deprive them of a grandchild. As a result, outside pressure to get pregnant is intense and the final reality of infertility often dramatic or disastrous.

Janice refused to believe her doctor's statement that if her surgery was successful she would become pregnant within six months. Instead, she continued beyond that time keeping her temperature chart, having sex at the specified time, and in the specific position. Finally, when passing a bookstore featuring a book on the joys of pregnancy, Janice stopped and the years of frustration took over. Janice cried right there, in the bookstore. "I did not care what anybody thought. I had waited a long time for that cry."

Betty recalls, after years of repeatedly unsuccessful surgeries, "The pressure had become so great that I offered my husband a divorce. I felt defective and unclean." Sadly, we hear many similar versions of Betty's story from both husbands and wives. It seems vulnerable spouses who view themselves as defective often feel compelled to free their mate by offering them a divorce.

For others the finality of an empty nursery and childlessness releases feelings of failure and hopelessness that take on dramatic proportions. "One night I felt I simply could not face another day," writes Kaye Halverson. "Pills, poisons, and car accidents kept flashing through my mind, and then the peace of death and joy of heaven."* Kaye subsequently worked through her crisis partly with the help of a national infertility support group—RESOLVE. This organization was started by infertile couples to offer counseling, referral, and support to others struggling to understand and accept infertility.

---

*Halverson, Kaye, with Karen M. Hess, *The Wedded Unmother*, Minneapolis, MN. Augsburg Publishing House, 1980.

APPROACHING ADOPTION

Not every couple resolves their infertility by seeking to adopt, nor should couples automatically believe adoption is their best or only alternative. Our work, of course, revolves primarily around adoption. Therefore, in this chapter we focus on couples who have opted for adoption rather than a childfree life. The following case history illustrates one such couple's initial approach to adoption and their subsequent evolution.

Ed and Marisa, ages 33 and 30, approached an adoption agency after seven years of marriage. They had been attempting unsuccessfully to have a child biologically for over three years. They initially had postponed starting a family so that Ed could finish his Ph.D. degree and secure a university teaching position. Marisa was also busy with her own career. When they finally decided to have a baby, they assumed Marisa would get pregnant immediately. When she didn't, they began the extensive and frustrating procedure of infertility testing. It seemed like an endless process, with month after month of disappointment. Marisa cried each month when her period started. She also found herself becoming easily depressed when friends became pregnant, and she began to question herself as a woman.

Both Ed and Marisa commented on the fact that up to this point in their lives they had been able to achieve anything they wanted, but now they felt powerless to achieve what they wanted most. When the doctor finally finished testing and found no reason for their infertility, he suggested adoption.

Initially Ed and Marisa were not sure they wanted to adopt. They wanted a child of their "own." As they discussed it repeatedly they realized that raising a child was more important to them than whether or not they gave birth. They decided to explore adoption. It was a little frightening, though, to make that first phone call. They were apprehensive about the mysterious agency and wondered if they had to be "perfect" in order to be accepted. After calling several agencies they learned that there is a nationwide shortage of Caucasian infants, compared to the large number of couples wanting to adopt. This made them feel even more nervous about measuring up to the obviously rigorous selection process.

When they reached the stage of an adoption home study, Ed and Marisa had feelings of ambivalence, nervousness, and hostility toward the agency—hostility at having to depend on strangers in order to have "their" child. They still felt the need to appear perfect to win the agency's approval. (It should be noted that Marisa and Ed worked with an agency that practiced semi-open adoption. Their agency assumed the traditional role of "decision maker," retaining power and control over most decisions. If Marisa and Ed had, instead, chosen an agency which focused on facilitating and empowering their clients, their adoption process would have been different and may have prevented or reduced some of the negative feelings they experienced.)

Through the adoption process at their agency, Marisa and Ed began to learn about the realities of adoption. They found themselves discussing adoption at home every day. They explored such emotionally charged issues as how they would feel about the birthparents, when and how they would start discussing adoption with their child, and what level of openness they would risk. They realized that before entering the adoption process, they had never thought about birthparents and their feelings. All their thoughts had been solely directed toward the baby.

They also talked to friends and relatives about adoptive issues. In discussing and thinking about adoption, they discovered that in spite of their fears and anger toward the agency's involvement in achieving parenthood, they had grown in the process. They felt better prepared to be parents, especially adoptive parents. Adoption seemed an acceptable way of forming a family. Now they knew that an adopted child would be their "own."

When they completed the home study process and their "Birthmother Letter," they were thrilled and relieved. They could simply look forward to the baby's arrival. This waiting period, however, also proved difficult. Marisa found herself waiting daily for the phone to ring. They soon began to wonder if they would ever get their call. Once more they were reminded that their destiny was out of their control.

Finally, they received "the call" about an already born baby girl. They excitedly drove to the agency to meet their new daughter, Kimberly. Again, they had some anxieties. They wondered if they would be good parents, if they would love Kimberly right away, and how they would feel if she were ugly. When they were presented a seven-day old baby girl with a full head of black hair, dark eyes, and fair skin, they both melted. This was the happiest moment of their married lives. They were filled with awe, excitement, and anticipation for their future.

Six months later during their social worker's last home visit, Ed and Marisa proudly showed off their daughter Kimberly and related all of her accomplishments. They felt sure she was the brightest, most beautiful baby ever! Both recalled that they hadn't experienced feelings of love instantly —in the beginning it sort of felt like they were babysitting some else's child. But as they cared for her day by day the feelings of love grew.

Once they had fully bonded with their new daughter, Ed and Marisa had some difficulty in remembering Kimberly's birthparents. They knew that these possessive feelings were natural because the baby was very much theirs, and it took a conscious effort to think of Kimberly's second set of parents. Ed and Marisa recalled that when they first discussed adoption, they had never thought about the individuals who would bear their child. They certainly had no appreciation of their feelings or their rights. It was as if they never existed. Yet, after the adoption education process and after exposure to numerous birthparents, they had grown to both understand and care for these two people. They reported that they were not threatened by Kimberly's birthparents. In fact, Ed and Marisa requested as much data and information about them as possible to ultimately share with their daughter. Ed and Marisa treasured the letters, pictures and gifts they received, because, "these items will be very special to Kimberly in later years." They both felt very comfortable and natural communicating with Kimberly's birthmother. "After all," they noted, "she has given us so much!"

Ed and Marisa's story is representative of couples seeking to become adoptive parents. Our experience with these couples has taught us that three distinct phases exist and must be addressed. Infertility resolution is one such critical phase. Resolving the childbearing loss dramatically parallels the same stages of grief as experienced when a family member dies (denial, anger, sadness, and finally acceptance). Regrettably, assistance in this area is often overlooked or summarily dealt with in most adoption programs.

We see as a second phase the adoption education process, which is an integral part of the adoption agency's program. For most adoptive parents this is an emotionally charged period because some other individual (either a social worker or the birthmother) has control of their fate. You will remember that Ed and Marisa experienced some natural anger at having to appear perfect to win agency approval.

The final phase involves the couple exploring the realities of adoptive parenthood. These realities focus on the adoptive family structure—its similarities to and differences from biological parenthood. As with Ed and Marisa, couples in this phase integrate their role without displacing the birthparents' place in the adoptee's life.

We will address in detail each of these three phases. Overall, the dynamics of what the couple faces can be best understood when viewed from the aspect of their lack of control or autonomy throughout their adoption experience. The first experience with loss of control (their infertility) is potentially the most draining. Being denied a natural child by infertility can be crippling unless the couple grows to accept this child's loss—this is both the first phase and the first struggle to become adoptive parents.

Couples vary in just how far they have progressed in accepting infertility when they first approach the adoption intermediary. Some are committed to adoption as their alternative to a child-free life. These couples may have even completed the process of mourning their never-to-be-born child. For these couples, an adoptive child is not a replacement but a child wanted for himself. Keith, a thirty-six-year-old adoptive father, explained this to the birthmother of his son in the following excerpt from his letter to her:

> Because my wife and I value our marriage, we
> have both taken the time and effort to make our

marriage a happy and giving relationship. One of the hardest periods of our marriage was when we desired to have children, but found out that we couldn't. It was extremely frustrating to see our friends and other people with their babies, and then realize that we couldn't have our own family. At first this was hard to accept. However, as soon as we realized that we were not able to have our own child, we immediately began inquiring into adoption and taking the necessary steps to adopt. The fact that my wife is adopted, together with the excellent and close relationship which she enjoys with her adoptive parents, made adoption very easy to accept. We did not consider adoption a last alternative, but instead merely a way of obtaining a baby that we wanted to have very much.

As his letter reflects, Keith and his wife decided not to lead a child-free life only after they had dealt with and accepted the fact their marriage would not produce that child. Their decision to adopt was motivated by a desire to experience parenthood.

By contrast, numerous couples begin the adoption process without first facing and dealing with the finality of their infertility. Although not one of our primary myths, a fiction widely believed by these couples and by their parents and friends is that "once you adopt, you will relax and have a child of your own." Therefore, rather than acknowledge their infertility, these couples pursue adoption in order to later obtain their desired pregnancy. Adoption is thus viewed as a temporary measure in their desperate quest for their "own" baby.

Wherever the couple may be in resolving their infertility, every couple approaching adoption benefits from the assistance of a professional adoption counselor. The adoption counselor must understand the vulnerability of these prospective parents, yet not overprotect them by avoiding painful topics. Couples need to accept the loss of their unborn child before they begin a relationship with the adoptee.

Resolution of infertility does not mean they will ever

forget that they could not bear their "own child," but it does mean they can see their adopted child for the individual he will become. They can also accept themselves without lingering feelings of failure, remorse, or anger. They can acknowledge the realities of adoptive parenthood without thinking they are second best to natural parents. To accomplish this, the couple must discuss openly their infertility experience, their grief, and their reasons for forming a family through adoption.

Adoption is not, of course, the only alternative for the infertile couple. If they do seek adoption, however, the adoptee must be wanted not as a "substitute" but as an individual who needs two parents to nurture, guide, and love him.

The second phase in assuming the role of adoptive parents involves the counseling and educational services provided by the professional adoption intermediary. Here, too, the empathy and wisdom of a trained intermediary is essential. In the case of traditional agency adoption, the couple believes their primary task is to convince an adoption social worker that they are stable, secure, and "together" people. Such a selling job allows the couple little time to explore the fears of adoptive parenthood such as, "Can we love someone else's child?" and "Will our parents accept an adopted grandchild?" or "What will our friends think?"

The couple might even find themselves unable to discuss with their social worker any deep seated fears they may have of becoming parents. Even final acceptance by an adoption agency does not end a couple's struggle or return control to them. Acceptance by the agency just begins a second long and often painful period of waiting. Although pregnancy also involves a waiting period, the two experiences are not similar. A husband and wife "expecting" a baby know their due date, and the time before the birth is accompanied by outward physical changes in the couple and society's approval. A husband and wife "awaiting" an adoptive placement do not know when their baby is due (or even how old that baby will be).

When an adoptive couple works with a progressive agency, in which the control is in the hands of the clients instead of the agency, they still have no due date, but they do not have to "prove themselves" to an agency social worker. This enables them to feel more in control of their own lives and their own adoption. Instead of assuming a passive role and waiting for the agency to call them, they are taking an active role, writing their "Birthmother Letter" and then distributing their letters through personal networking efforts in the hopes of locating a birthmother.

Society, in addition, does not assist the adoptive couple in preparing for their role change to parenthood. Even family members and friends may not provide approving support to the adopting couple. This can be partly explained because the couple shows no outward signs that they will soon be parents. More significant, however, is the general lack of understanding about adoption. Since most of those around us tenaciously believe the four myths of adoption, individual reactions will vary to a couple's decisions to adopt. There are those around the adopting couple who anxiously verbalize a fear that the "birthmother will reclaim her child." Others are over-solicitous in their support, "Gee, you are really special to adopt someone else's child. I don't think I could." Finally, some are unknowingly cruel, "You're so lucky—adopting is the easy way of having a child." All these comments and subtle messages motivate the couple to regain control of their life—free from scrutiny—once the baby is actually placed in their arms.

When placement day finally arrives, we hear many couples talk of their compulsion "to get my baby out of this agency (or hospital) and home." Their urgent need is to escape to the sanction and privacy of their home, "dress him in his own clothes," and thus regain control of their life and family. Pain from the loss of any biological child and the frustration of outside scrutiny has extended over a long period.

Once adoptive parents do have their long awaited child in their home, they are tempted to pretend or forget he was adopted. Nanette, an adoptive mother describes it best in this way:

> Intellectually, I know that the baby was adopted, but emotionally I can pretend that he has been and is totally mine in every way.

Pretending as if the adoptive child was born naturally to the couple is common and takes many forms. Frequently, the couples working with us speak of a type of complete (yet innocent appearing) denial, "I keep forgetting he was adopted." Other couples describe their "as if" attitude as follows, "I have always considered Andrew adopted, but I have never really seen myself as an adoptive mother."

No matter the form, adoptive parents living this pretense are seeking to be normal parents. Seeking to be normal really means denying that they first had to go through the infertility nightmare and then suffer through the adoption process. Another part of the need for this "as if" pretense is a desire for societal and familial acceptance and approval. Because myths create misconceptions and apprehensions among family members, friends, and the neighborhood grocery clerk, the adoptive couple soon learns it is easier not to mention adoption. A frequent comment among adoptive parents is, "I get tired of answering questions—insensitive questions that often hurt."

The final contributor to a couple's need to pretend is the largely unconscious feeling that the child's birthparents are his "real mother and father." Considering the work it took to become parents, some adoptive couples fear the day their child might decide to search for his "true" parents (fourth myth). Overall, this pretense results in more feelings of helplessness, sadness, and defeat.

THE REALITIES OF ADOPTIVE PARENTHOOD

We see the final phase of becoming an adoptive parent as accepting the realities of this form of parenthood. In effect, this means progressing from pretending that the child was born naturally to the couple to the pain-free integration of the realities of adoption. Here our approach revolves around sensitizing adoptive parents to three often blunt concepts:

1. **Adoption is a lifetime experience.** (It does not go away when the intermediary contact is over.)

2. **Adoptive parents will never totally parent their**

child; and adoptees will never be totally parented by their adoptive parents. (There are no "as if" pretenses allowed.)

3. **Birthparents remain a part of the adoptee's life** whether physically separated or reunited.

Adoption Is a Lifetime Experience

The first reality acknowledges that escaping into the home after the child's placement does not erase how the family was formed. Although the temptation exists to forget the entire adoption process, such forgetting is potentially harmful to the child and to the family structure. Given the need and drive for candor in relationships today, adoptive parents have a responsibility to tell the child he was adopted and to subsequently keep communication channels open. Information from the adoption experience belongs, in part, to the child and his evolving identity. This requires a conscious commitment by the couple not to forget, and a resource commitment from adoption intermediaries and post-adoption programs (post-adoption programs offer the ongoing educational and counseling support necessary when one acknowledges that adoption is a lifetime experience).

The following letter from Bob and Linda was written shortly after their daughter was placed in their arms. Feelings expressed to their daughter's birthmother demonstrate their commitment to base their relationship on truth and openness. They know that for the five people involved (birthparents, adoptive parents, and child) adoption is a lifetime experience:

> Dear Special Person,
>
> Through this letter we hope to communicate some of our feelings at this very special time of our lives. Although we realize there is no way we could ever express all the great joy we have experienced since adopting our precious little girl.
>
> We always wanted children, but discovered we would not be biological parents. We knew we would love a child—being biological wasn't important.

After being accepted by the agency, we were excited and filled with anticipation. We made all necessary preparations—wallpapered nursery, bought furnishings, took a child care course, read parenting materials, and anxiously waited for our special day. By this time we knew we would have a baby soon and we knew we would love this child. But, we never realized how much!

Our little adopted girl is our whole world. We can't imagine life without her. She has enriched our lives so much. We feel she is the perfect child for us. We are very much a family. She is ours and we are hers. In addition to all our love, she is loved by four grandparents, who are all young and actively involved in her life. . . .

At this happy time in our lives, we realize that this is a difficult time of your life. Upon placement we cried many tears of joy for us and tears of sadness for you. We know you sacrificed you own feelings for your child's future. You are truly a special person. Our daughter will know she's adopted and will know you are out there somewhere. She will only hear positive things about you. She will never be told that you did not want her or love her, rather it was because you loved her so much that you gave her up. There will always be a special place in our hearts for you. You are a special person. God bless and keep you always.

Love,
Parents of An Angel

Adoptive Parents Will Never Totally Parent

The second reality—never being able to totally parent the adoptee—is initially the hardest to present to adopting parents. Introducing this concept always produces the same startled and defensive comment, "What do you mean TOTALLY parent?"

Not being able to totally parent does not say anything about the adoptive couple's ability to love or be "together people." There are no first or second-best parents in this human experience. There are only adoptive parents who can never give their biological heritage or genetic future to their child and birthparents who can not raise a child born to them. Both sets of parents in reality experience an incompleteness and loss. The child, in turn, can never be parented by *one set* of parents. He needs the adoptive set to provide the nurturing and shaping part of parenthood. He needs the biological set to provide his genetic past and future.

An adoptive couple's initial defensiveness to the idea that they may not be total parents stems in part from their own belief that the child's birthparents are not only the child's "real" parents, but also the "complete" parents. Complete refers to the ability of the birthparents to have successfully reproduced themselves. The uniquely important experience of passing on one's family genes is, of course, not duplicated in the adoptive family structure.

Our discussions with adoptive couples concerning this aspect of the realities focus on how lack of a blood-bond to the adoptee can lead parents to feel sadness, fear, and anger at times. Couples have described experiences of feeling like second-best parents. A parent who feels he is somehow second-best to his child's birthparents and other real parents in this world is apt to put his need to compete with the birthparents above the child's need for knowledge about his heritage. This same adoptive parent may unconsciously seek to totally possess the child instead of helping him integrate information about his birthparents into his growing self-concept.

When adoption intermediaries or well-intentioned friends attempt to minimize for adoptive parents the importance of genetically related birthparents, both parents and children are the real losers. Such statements as, "the nurturing part of parenting is the BEST part of parenthood," are unjust because they encourage adoptive parents to remain defensive. If adoptive parents experience competitive feelings towards birthparents, we believe these feelings are best explored before they adopt. This allows adoptive parents to develop greater insight into themselves and the true importance of their role.

Samantha and Charles, a young adoptive couple,

understand and accept this second reality. No matter how hard they may wish, they will never totally parent their son, Jimmy. They can, however, be secure with themselves as Jimmy's parents—secure enough to invite Jimmy's birthmother, Candace, to be a part of their life. Candace, in turn, writes the following letter. All five people in this adoption drama win because they were helped to deal with their initial fears, and then to grow through open communication and trust. Jimmy now has access to both sets of parents:

Samantha and Charles,

I want to thank you for the beautiful ceramic box. I really love it. I was very excited when I was told I had a letter from you and don't worry it was worth waiting for.

I am so glad Jimmy is doing so well. I have always been told that adopted children take on characteristics of their adoptive parents or I should say parents. I think Jimmy will grow up that way. I hope you are keeping a baby book on him. I think that adds something. I know I'm prejudiced, but he is the handsomest boy in the world. If I ever have any more children he will still be my prettiest one.

My life is passing by in an unremarkable way. I am trying to sort out my life and see where I am going. So far it isn't very far. I am planning on school. The next semester is June which is a long time from now.

Do you know what is very difficult? I work in a Pediatrics office and everyone brings their babys here. Maybe God chose this for me to help me over the rough spots. I can't hide here. I still feel very comfortable with what has happened. I don't really feel cheated. Sort of detached is a better way of saying it.

I should tell you I had hardly any hair until I was almost two. Now I sit on it. It grows very quickly. I also have a very bad temper and when I was younger I could not control it. I use to do the whole bit of laying on the floor and kicking. And people learn very quickly not to cross me. I am much better now and I am sure Jimmy will out grow his. By the way, I have never been able to sleep while in a moving vehicle, plane or car. I sleep only when not moving. Maybe Jimmy is that way. I am so glad the family enjoyed him.

I have everything from the time Jimmy was in the hospital. I have an envelope that I keep everything in. Your letters and pictures are there.

Well you two take care of each other and Jimmy. I hope things go well.

Love,
Candace

Birthparents Remain a Part of the Adoptee's Life

We often hear adoptive parents say that simply telling the child he was adopted is all they felt was necessary. The idea of mentioning birthparents or the concept that the child would be curious had not occurred to them. The third reality is thus designed to equip adoptive parents with this essential information.

The fact that birthparents remain a part of the adoptee's life, whether physically separated or reunited, emphasizes the bond that exists between a child and his birthparents. Whether described as a family connection or blood tie, adoptees tell us that this bond plays a role in their lives. Some adoptees speak of this role as merely an intellectual curiosity about their background, while other adoptees verbalize an emotional drive to have physical contact with a blood relative. At either extreme, the adoptee would like to be able to share his feelings with his adoptive parents. The adoptive parents, however, can both envy and fear the importance of this blood-bond to their child, which may make communication difficult or impossible.

Adoptees frequently mention the importance of such simple questions as what their birthparents' personalities were like, what were their interests, what did they look like, but most especially, "Did my birthparents love me?" It is our belief that adoptive parents have a duty to convey whatever facts they know. In addition, it is the responsibility of the adoptive parents to let the adoptee know that they are comfortable in answering his questions—that in fact they expect him to ask questions. Failure to freely communicate may prevent the adoptee from exploring his identity. Whereas, a comfortable, open attitude may prevent a great deal of anxiety and guilt.

Once again, our approach is to introduce to the adoptive parents the reality of the birthparents' continued role in the adoptee's life, and then assist them to understand how that role and their role merge in the child's life. Adoptive parents who are comfortable with this last reality make a double achievement. Because they are capable of empathizing with the child's need to know his blood-bond, they will not feel the pain of rejection if he does decide to search for his birthparents. Most important, the adoptive parents can free the adoptee from any disquieting yearning about himself, and possibly earn the reward of being his favored lifetime partners in all his important searches.

LEARNING THROUGH LETTERS

Letter exchanges make it possible for adopting couples to shape and resolve their feelings about the realities of their parental status. We find they write about who they are today and how their infertility experience and adoption struggle helped them grow and mature. They also face their greatest fear—their child's birthparents—in an open manner. As adoptive parents share their life with these birthparents, they come to understand how and why birthparents are a part of the adoptee's life. They also demonstrate confidence in themselves which is then reflected in a relaxed and loving family unit. For example, Rob and Elaine had been married thirteen years before becoming adoptive parents. The period of *becoming* parents held times of real depression for them both. In the following excerpts from the letter they wrote shortly after placement, they share with their child's birthmother their struggle not only to assume their role but also to accept it:

Dear Birth Mother,

We were so happy to receive your nice letter and it will be saved for our daughter. Even though we have not met you we are united in a deep bond of love with you for this beautiful child. Her birth into this world is one of the most wonderful events that has ever happened. The events in all of our lives that have taken place within the past year will provide new and even more beautiful meanings as time goes by. We know that life can be very difficult at times for each of us and we know so clearly from personal experiences what it is like to struggle and suffer and ask ourselves why we have to go through such times. We now believe that these events are part of a process of learning, growing and developing into stronger persons than we may have ever dreamed was possible for us. Because of this precious child's life we all find new meanings to the word love. We want you to know that there has never been a child born that is more dearly loved nor one who has brought more joy into a home than this little girl. We believe you made very mature and good decisions. We also believe that the Lord is guiding your life and making it possible for you to experience and have a wonderful life filled with love.

We share your great love and respect for this child's life. Since she came into our lives many wonderful and surprising things have taken place. Family, friends and acquaintances from all over the country have written to us—special notes have even been written just for her. She has been given many, many lovely toys, clothes and things that a baby needs. We never expected such an overwhelming outpouring of friendship and love from so many people. It has truly been a thrilling and exciting experience. This is one of the reasons why we say that her life has already shown us love and what wonderful love there is in this world. . . .

We are very proud and happy to be her Mother

and Father, and we believe you can be proud also. We wish to have you understand and to feel the great sense of satisfaction, joy and love that her life has brought to us. It is not possible to say in one letter what a miracle she is to us.

We pray for you and want you to have faith, joy and love in your life, increasing as time goes by. We send you our love and our very best wishes for a wonderful life.

Love,
The Adoptive Parents

Another couple, Patricia and Fred, wrote three letters to their child's birthmother within the first three years. Their third letter demonstrates their evolution and final acceptance of the realities involved in adoption. They reached this point by continuing to read books on adoption, by attending workshops about adoption, by remaining active in an adoptive parent support group, as well as by going through the adoption process again for a second child:

Dear Birthmother,

Greetings! I was so happy to hear from our social worker that you and she had spoken. I am so glad that all is well with you. I will try to bring you up to date on the happenings in this last year. It has been a hectic one since we are now the parents of two daughters. As you can imagine, being the parents of two is more complicated plus hectic than being the parents of one!

We have really enjoyed watching the love develop between the two sisters. As the older and more mature sister, Katherine gives the baby lots of guidance, loving care, and needless to say, bossing! Katherine knows how to feed her and does try to be helpful whenever she gets a chance or whenever she's in the mood for it. . . .

It has been terrific to watch Katherine's development and reasoning ability. She is extremely intelligent and quick. She talks in complete sentences and has done so for over a year. Her vocabulary is excellent—she uses words like delicate, initiated and wonderful. She has good command of shades of meanings and abstract words. . . .

I am enclosing some pictures for you. I will get some more duplicated for you. Please do be patient, tho, because it usually takes me awhile to do things these days.

I really appreciate your being willing to fill out the form our agency has devised for sharing additional information. I want you to know that we would love to hear any and all details about you and your family. We want Katherine to feel there is continuity in her life and we don't want her heritage to be a mystery. As I have learned more about adoption I have come to realize how important all this is. We would love to have names, birthdates, places of birth, pictures and anything else you feel like sharing about you, your family, and anyone else you feel would feature as important in Katherine's life. She is so atuned to adoption that it's just terrific. When she was about 2-1/2 she pensively asked me "Mommy, my birthmother, she not know me?" I went on to explain that you did know her at birth and that you did spend time with her. Isn't it amazing how quickly children grasp information?!

Well, as you can see I can go on and on about Katherine. . . .

We think of you often and feel so fortunate that we are Katherine's parents. She is a joy! And I am sure that some day you will have the opportunity to see that first hand. As our social worker mentioned to you if ever you would like to talk on the phone or in person with me, I would be very delighted to meet you. It would be marvelous to be able to share with Katherine personal contact with you. Again, it takes the mystery out of adoption and truly personalizes it. For as someone (an adoptive parent) recently wrote to her child's birthmother

"Tho he is our child now, he will never stop being your child too." We feel that way too. I want you to know that as long as you want a yearly letter regarding Katherine, that I will be very happy to write you one. I must admit that it is fun to go on and on about her!

Stay well. We too would love to hear from you and do stay in touch.

All the best to you.

> With great fondness,
> Patricia

Through the letter exchange, couples like Rob and Elaine and Patricia and Fred find themselves not fearing some invisible birthparent. Instead, adoptive parents speak in caring terms of "our" birthparents. As a result, couples naturally progress from a need to pretend that the child was born to them to an acceptance of the adoptive family structure as it is.

Adoption is not a onetime event that otherwise mimics biological parenthood. There are differences—differences that do not have to overpower any couple if openly and honestly managed. Since we have used this approach, we have seen the struggle to accept infertility end in both growth and peace for our adoptive parents.

6
The Adoption Intermediary: Preparing The New Parents

It's my child's birthday today
I have no memories of the pain and struggle,
as he entered this life
As he fought for his first breath
I have no memories of his life growing inside of me
and fighting to be released
I have no memories from the beginning months of
his life.
Another "someone" was there—Another "someone"
suffered for my joy . . . *

Today's intermediary in the adoption process is doing a significantly better job than ever before—but there is still much to be done. The work is too crucial to leave to half measures and happenstance. Let's start with our philosophy of the intermediary role:

> The professional adoption counselor, agency, doctor, or lawyer provides not just a mechanical function of placing a child (or facilitating the placement), but must be an aid in *preparing* the adoptive parents and birthparents for a new role. Furthermore, the intermediary must empower the adoptive parents (and birthparents) to be in control

---

* From "A Birthday," reprinted with permission of the author from Adoption Triangle Ministry.

of the adoption. We firmly believe *all* of the decisions and choices must be in the hands of the parties involved, not the adoption intermediary. The
intermediary role must be one of providing counseling, education, and support, rather than control
and decision making.

In this chapter, we will explore how we have applied the
above ideology to our work with prospective adoptive parents. Later, in Chapter 7, we will examine this philosophy in
reference to our adoptive practices with birthparents.

BEYOND SCREENING: COUNSELING AND HOME STUDY

Couples readily seek an intermediary to adopt a child, but
less commonly to obtain assistance in integrating their role as
adoptive parents. Knowing the dual purpose of an intermediary, responsible intermediaries must help the potential adoptive parents in both areas and not serve simply as a
"screening" agency. Regrettably, traditional adoptive home
studies revolve only around the screening process and the
suitability of the prospective parents as parents. Investigation
of the home and family circumstances all too often leave off
before making the most important inquiry. Areas unique to
adoptive parenthood are often neglected in the search for a
"perfect couple."

One prospective adoptive couple, Martin and Sheila,
had been "approved" for adoption by two agencies within the
past two years. Each time Martin and Sheila moved to another
area before a child could be placed with them. In reading the
completed home studies from these other two well-known
agencies, we discovered thorough descriptions of the couple, their personalities, marital adjustments, family background, and experience with children. We found no
references to how Martin and Sheila would tell their child he
was adopted, how they felt about the unique responsibilities
of adoptive parenthood, or what they thought or felt toward
the potential birthparents of their child. In short, neither
agency had discussed adoption.

Martin is an attorney and Sheila is a nurse and both admit they believed the intermediary's sole objective was to screen and approve of them as parents. They did not see beyond the baby stages of diapers and feeding. They did not anticipate, nor did the intermediary alert them, to the time when the inevitable issues of adoptive parenthood would arise. Martin and Sheila were even unaware that the role of an adoptive parent required additional preparation. Like most couples, Martin and Sheila did not know any other adoptive couples who might have answered questions or served as role models. Actually, their entire knowledge and experience about adoption consisted of the four myths plus the unusual but scarcely enlightening experience of what we can only characterize as two superficial studies into their suitability to adopt a child.

Martin and Sheila are typical. The intermediary—whether professional counselor, agency, family physician, or lawyer—is approached by two vulnerable individuals who possess limited or faulty insight into the implications of the role they seek. Adoption, to these frustrated potential parents, may be their only way to get a child and to regain control of their lives and destinies. They do not know the realities of adoption; and they certainly do not know the questions that will be most important to prepare them to be effective adoptive parents.

When the professional intermediary merely places a child with such a "perfect couple," the intermediary effectively encourages the couple to consider the child "as if" he were theirs by natural birth. As we point out in Chapter 5, forgetting the differences in how the family was formed is an understandable adaptation to a long and painful infertility experience. Besides, without trained intermediary assistance and support, the adopting parents learn no other options.

If this couple is later introduced to the realities of adoption, they will be surprised and frightened. No knowledgeable intermediary is there to explain or reassure, and the realities, which we have already discussed, are blunt:

1. Adoption is a lifetime experience.
2. Adoptive parents will never totally parent their child;

and adoptees will never be totally parented by their adoptive parents.

3. Birthparents remain a part of the adoptee's life whether physically separated or reunited.

These realities, combined with the misconceptions of the myths and any unresolved issues around infertility, create a dissonance that makes moving toward open ideas very difficult, if not insurmountable.

In contrast, our work with prospective adoptive parents acknowledges that the burden of preparing these parents for their new role rests always with the intermediary. We believe that the primary role of the intermediary is to provide counseling, education about adoption issues and realities, and support. We want our couples to explore their stereotypes, misconceptions and apprehensions before they become parents.

Our first objective is to expose the four myths of adoption as harmful and stultifying. We recommend beginning this process at the Orientation Meeting, which is the adopting couple's initial introduction to the realities in adoption. This session explores the myths and realities in adoption, as well as the benefits of open adoption.

Couples who enter our adoption program attend an intensive adoption workshop. This workshop typically includes eight to ten prospective adoptive couples and a group leader. The group leader acts as a facilitator since the workshop stresses group exploration and discussion, not lectures. Activities are designed to allow all participants to examine feelings about their infertility experience and their beliefs about birthparents. Required reading also expands the couple's awareness of adoption issues.

Initial discussions, for example, explore the attitudes of our prospective parents about the role they are seeking— adoptive parenthood. Where are they in the process of resolving infertility? Is this baby to be a substitute for the natural child they have been denied? Do they believe genuine parenthood is the child-bearing-and-rearing type only? What do they know about adoption? Which of the four myths do they believe? Which of the four myths do their parents and friends believe? This discussion area acknowledges the differences between biological and adoptive parenthood, and initiates an inspection by all participants of their own attitudes towards adoption and themselves as adoptive parents.

An important aspect of the workshop focuses on understanding the birthparents. Do our adopting couples imagine the birthmother as a "tramp," and the birthfather as "irresponsible?" How will they tell their child his birthparents were unmarried? Does it matter to them, to their family, to their friends that the child may be illegitimate? Discussions stress that each adoptive parent's feelings toward the birthparents will affect the child's evolving self image.

We climax our introduction to the realities of birthparents through a panel of actual birthmothers who have placed their babies for adoption. These birthmothers talk about their feelings towards pregnancy, their decision to place their babies for adoption, their ongoing relationship with the adoptive family and child, and each one's love for her child. This leads to couples asking the birthmothers further questions about their experiences. This dialogue is undoubtedly the richest part of the workshop, and something the couples vividly remember.

The following letter from Bob, expresses some of his initial apprehensions about open adoption and his personal evolution as the result of the workshop experience:

> My only reason for selecting an open adoption was to get a baby. The closed systems no longer had children readily available, and after six years of the infertility circus my wife and I wanted a lovely little baby <u>right now.</u> Other than that I had no reason for choosing an open adoption as an option. The whole concept of "open" seemed too radical and unstable for my more traditional concept of adoption—"give me the child, seal the records, and get lost." The fact that the child had birthparents was irrelevant to me. Their presence represented more of a liability to me than an asset, a threat more than anything. What if they changed their mind? What if they want to come and see the baby? Do they want to spend Christmas with us? Why don't they just go

sway? Will my child love me if the birthparents are around? My selfish and narrow minded hostility to these questions almost prevented me from adopting my little daughter Kate.

I was blinded by the idea that I knew all about adoption. Little did I realize that I was prejudging the entire process without taking the time to understand the nature of adoption itself. Fortunately, the Independent Adoption Center required that I participate in a series of sessions structured to familiarize me with the many aspects of open adoption. It was at these sessions that I began to realize how narrow my thinking was and how many of the things I was most fearful of were simply rooted in mistrust, lack of control, and ignorance. My fears were dissipated by the many people who spoke about their happiness and success. They made me see that the more open the adoption the greater the benefit for all concerned.

By knowing the birthparents I will be able to deal openly with the many questions that will inevitably be faced. Medical information only begins to scratch the surface of what I need to know. I began to realize that by pretending that there are no birthparents, or that ignorance was bliss, I was building a new life and family on a lie. I could not make a biological family out of an adoptive one, and that was an unpalatable truth to accept.

Lastly I had to respect the birthparents' desire to place this child in a home of their choosing. Adoption was a choice that they wanted. Ironically we were all on the same side, solving each others problem. As for the little requests by a birthmother to come and see the baby once in a while, well that was no longer the threat it used to be. Once I made the effort to understand the birthmother's desire to have this adoption succeed, that's when I realized how small a request she was making. She was giving us a gift for a lifetime. Her decision made possible a dream of ours that all the science in the world could not satisfy. Once I appreciated how much she was doing for us, I found it hard not to have the compassion and love to care for her needs, too.

The workshop is designed to sensitize participants to how their own infertility experience will play a part in their role as adoptive parents. In addition, activities are designed to illustrate how their myths, stereotypes, or expectations could shape their judgments about birthparents and adoptees. Couples often begin the workshop convinced that anyone who gives away a child could not love that child (first myth), and neither wants nor deserves information about the child (third myth). Many couples at this stage freely admit that they fear the birthparents as a threat to the family unit they so desperately desire. This mixture of misconceptions, untruths, and anxieties is revealed and discussed during the workshop.

This next sensitive letter was written by Hugh and Jane to their son's birthmother. The letter is significant because Hugh had entered the workshop with strong negative preconceptions about all birthparents. His attitude is familiar: "What right does she have to information? After all she obviously did not want the baby; she gave it away." In contrast, their letter demonstrates an ability to empathize with the birthmother after only a short exposure to the birthparent's perspective:

Dear Birth Mother of Our Son,

Through the grace of God, you brought a precious son into this world. His life has already brought so much joy to so many! If things are truly planned, this could not have been more perfectly planned. He has fit into our lives as if it was always meant to be. He has also brought so much happiness to our families and friends. There has been more excitement over this beautiful child than we have ever seen for such an important occasion.

Most importantly, we want you to know

what a wonderfully beautiful little person he is.
Our son is growing in all ways—physically, emotionally, intellectually and spiritually. We know we
have someone in our home that we will be a
tremendous influence on, but we will do the very
best we can to raise him as an individual in his
own right.

Our son is a very happy little guy, with a
sunny disposition. His smile and laugh is worth
more than all the riches in the world. He is healthy,
well-adjusted, very alert, attentive, and strong. He
babbles, coos, talks, sings, and blows millions of
happy bubbles! He notices everything around him
with great interest, and loves to go outdoors and
take walks in his stroller.

We sit with him in our laps and look at books
with him, and he is already fascinated. We listen to
a lot of music, and deep-voiced singing is his
favorite. In the car we play a Harry Chapin tape he
is especially attentive to... Thank you for all the
gifts you sent (though, here those words seem too
small!) We will keep all of them as wonderful
remembrances. The night light is burning continu-
ously by his crib. The mobile is just beautiful, and
fits perfectly in his bright, sunny room. Please
thank your friend for it.

Yes, he was born in the year of the Child, and
came to us in the year of the Family. We want you
to know that he will know he had a birthmother
who loved him very much. Thank you from his
adoptive parents who love him more than words
can ever say. Thank you for giving him life—thank
you for entrusting that life to us. We love him truly
for himself, and we love you.

Our son will be baptised on Easter Sunday—
what a perfect time for this child of God!

May God bless and keep you. May you find joy
and love in this world, and know the joy and love
you have given others. You will always be in our
hearts and prayers; please remember us in yours.

You are very special. You gave us all something no
one else could.

Love from all of us,
His Adoptive Parents

Finally, the workshop focuses on some other adoption
realities and on the remaining individual in the adoption
drama—the adoptee. Our objectives at this point are two. The
first objective is to create an encouraging and supportive
atmosphere so the adoptive parents may examine any
unconscious needs to compete with the child's birthparents.
This drive to compete often masquerades in the second myth
(secrecy is the only way) and fourth myth (adoptees should
not search). Our objective is to uncover the competitiveness
and provide information to show that adoptive parents are not
second-best parents.

In addition, we assist these prospective parents to leave
behind the tendency to see and believe what they want to see
and believe, especially the "as if he were born to me" adaptation. With support from a group atmosphere, we present the
three primary realities of adoption: This is a lifetime commitment; you are not the adoptee's only parents; and birthparents remain part of your life because they are a part of the
adoptee.

Our second objective is to help participants prepare the
child to face life with an open, informed, relaxed acceptance
of the fact he was adopted. Adoption should be a natural and
comfortable subject in the home. If the adoptee grows up
always knowing he was adopted, he will consider the subject
commonplace. Results may be quite different, however, if he
learns of his adoptive status for the first time at later periods
of emotional development.

Throughout this session, adoptive parents are shown
how their attitudes will reflect in their communications to their
child. The dynamics are simple. As the child begins to question the adoption process and his "other parents," adoptive
parents can once again become unsure of their worth as parents and angry at these mysterious birthparents. Parents so
hurt and threatened may answer questions in such a way as
to block further questions. If mother stumbles with her answer

and tears come to her eyes, the adoptee quickly gets the message not to ask.

Young children unable to talk about adoption will often display anxieties, nightmares, fantasies, or behavioral problems. In addition, we often meet adoptive parents of older adoptees who say, "My child doesn't want to know anything. He is perfectly content." Sadly, their son may be actively but secretly searching for his birthparents but unable to share his search with his parents because he does not want to hurt them. Open communication in the home can eliminate or reduce these problems for both young and older adoptees. Therefore, through the workshop experience we teach our parents that open communication must be a conscious goal of each adoptive parent.

As mentioned earlier, adoptive parents tend to forget how the adoptee came into their family once they become a family unit. The stage could thus be set for these parents not to tell the adoptee at all. Allison, an adoptive mother who is herself an adoptee, understands the perils involved. She remembers growing up, "always knowing I was adopted." She plans on her son also having all the information he will need: "I hope that we will be able to make him feel as secure in our love for him as my parents made me feel." Allison wrote this reassuring letter to the birthmother of her son:

> To the Birth Mother of Our Son,
>
> First, I would like to thank you for the very beautiful letters you sent to us and our son. I know that someday they will be very meaningful to him and will help him to understand his adoption.
>
> I would like to tell you a little about myself. I, too, was adopted. I was born in San Antonio. However, since my Dad was in the service I spent most of my growing years all over the world. Our family is extremely close knit. I have a brother and sister, also adopted. Our parents are truly wonderful people and we have always felt very loved and very secure. My mother and father were very open and honest with us about the circumstances of our adoption. I never felt that I was unwanted and I

know that my son will understand why you could not care for him. . . .

I have so many feelings I would like to express to you. Compassion—I know your decision to give your baby up for adoption was a difficult one. I admire your courage and respect you for doing what you felt to be in the best interest of your baby. I am extremely grateful to you for giving us a beautiful son for our own. . . .

His disposition couldn't be better. He seldom gets fussy or cries. He's just a happy little baby. I can attribute his disposition in part to the peace you felt with yourself during your pregnancy. Your letters seemed to convey that you were peaceful with your decision. We take him everywhere and he is always good. For Thanksgiving, we took him to Dallas to meet my husband's family. They were thrilled with him and each one took their turn holding him and bouncing him on their knee. For Christmas he met my side of the family. My mother was the only one who saw him right away and she came as soon as we got him. His homecoming was her birthday. The whole family was quite taken with him and his grandfather just sat and marvelled at him. . . .

What else can I tell you? From the very first moment that I held him, I loved him and felt he was mine. Each day that I wake up and look at him, I can hardly believe it. Our love for him grows stronger each day and we enjoy watching him develop.

I have saved all the information and papers regarding his adoption and birth to place in a scrapbook. I intend to put it in storybook form, so that he will have his own little story. I hope that we will be able to make him feel as secure in our love for him as my parents made me feel.

I could go on and on, but there are really not enough appropriate words to express my feelings. I love our beautiful son and I will have a special place in my heart for the woman who made my dreams become a reality.

Thank you.

The workshop ends with a role-playing exercise designed to introduce the couples to questions an adopted child might ask. Questions range from a three-year-old asking, "Was I in your tummy, Mommy?" to a six-year-old asking "Why did my 'real' Mommy give me up?" The role-playing prevents the couples from simply intellectualizing about adoption and instead directs energies to the difficult experiences of actually sharing information with the child.

The entire workshop is an emotional experience for adopting couples. The group leader must remain creative in order to facilitate interaction by everyone. This effort requires a commitment of time and energy by the adoption intermediary. The work is rewarded by the growth and happiness experienced by the couples, and vividly demonstrated in their letters:

To the Mother of our Dear Child,

While this letter is not hard to write in the sense that you are our baby's natural mother, it is difficult in the respect that we could never be able to put down on paper the absolute happiness and joy he has brought to us. As we write this letter in the early morning, he is lying between us on the bed gurgling and laughing and enjoying us as we enjoy him. He is without a doubt the sweetest thing on this earth, and we fear he will be just a little bit spoiled but we're not going to worry about that. He's the first grandchild and the first niece or nephew for four of his uncles and aunt; he's the star of the show wherever he goes. We're lucky also that three of our dearest friends have children close to his age or will have children within the next several months—so he'll be part of a loving family and close friendships. His grandfather stops by every morning on his way to work to bring him a freshly cut rose and to play with him.

I hope this letter doesn't sound disjointed or rambling, but there are so many things we'd like to relate to you that they just seem to come in flashes.

To sum up his characteristics—if there is a cuter or smarter baby than he, a person would be hard pressed to find him or her. A little parental pride showing through but we feel that way. We don't want to sound gushy, but he is just about the sweetest thing to happen to us.

We know how difficult it was for you to part with him, and your letter touched us deeply. We believe that someone with your sensitivity and love must have passed that to your child, and we will be eternally grateful. You may not know how someone can love a child who is not theirs naturally, but rest assured it seems to be the most natural thing of all—loving a sweet and beautiful innocent. The minute we saw him at the agency, it was love at first sight and it has grown by leaps and bounds.

We were raised in close loving families and we know the value of love and its overt expressions, so we take every opportunity to hold, hug, or kiss him—it's so easy to do with him.

In ending this letter, we would want you to know that he is secure and loved and will be for the rest of our lives.

Sincerely yours,
The Adoptive Parents

A POST-ADOPTION COMMITMENT

During the post-placement stage, couples are encouraged to attend regularly scheduled post-birth group counseling sessions. These sessions, which are led by a counselor, focus again on adoption issues and realities—now from the perspective of actually being adoptive parents and having "real" birthparents to relate to.

Even that does not end our story. We work to keep couples involved with the adoption center after their adoption is final. Through a volunteer alumni group, we sponsor an annual family picnic (which many adoptive parents attend with their birthmother), annual banquet, and numerous other family activities throughout the year (e.g. a trip to the zoo, Easter egg hunt, etc.). The picnic, as well as other family activities, serves to bring couples back together to proudly show off their children and to jointly celebrate their happiness.

We also encourage adoptive families to become volunteers with our organization. Volunteers serve a variety of capacities, including office work, transporting birthmothers to the office for counseling appointments, housing a birthmother, etc. Through interaction with adoptive parents, birthmothers see what an adoptive family is like while still making their own decisions about adoption; and in turn, the families gain valuable further understanding of birthparents.

We also see the need for agencies and other adoption organizations to focus on post-finalization services. Ongoing workshops and support groups should be available for adoptive parents, birthparents, adoptees, and interested professionals to help each face questions and problems in dealing with adoption in the years after the child's placement. We are very pleased to know resources are available today to deal with the realities of adoption. In many ways, we see forward-looking adoption intermediaries agreeing with Lorraine, the adoptive mother who wrote the following in a letter to her son's birthmother:

> . . . God, through you and our son's birthfather, has answered our prayers in bringing to us a bright ray of sunshine in the form of our sweet little boy. We all share a special bond . . . we will have each given of ourselves to the creation of this very special little person.

7
The Adoption Intermediary: Preparing the Birthparents

Fly away—fly away
Never to return
I've lost
and you've gained.

There's an empty feeling deep inside
A warm spot—growing cold
These feelings I've accepted
Hoping one day they be filled.

Fly away—fly away
Never to return
I've lost
And you've gained.

There was an empty feeling deep inside
Now a cold spot—growing warm
These feelings being accepted
Gaining happiness and love.
        D. L. Click
        Birthmother

Birthparents confronted with an unplanned pregnancy face both the stress of an immediate crisis and the possibility of lifetime pain. For the birthmother three options challenge her, each emotionally charged:

> "Do I seek an abortion?"
> "Do I give birth and then raise my child?"
> "Do I place my child for adoption?"

Birthfathers and immediate family members also deal with each of these alternatives but from a perspective more physically removed. Adoption is only one of the alternatives for all these individuals, and not necessarily the "only good and reasonable choice." Contrary to the overwhelming belief in the myths of adoption that say birthparents "do not care" and birthparents "will and should forget," birthparents care deeply for the life they create.The decision to relinquish that life for someone else to parent is an unforgettable decision. This decision can result in a lifetime of grief and despair, the trauma of which some birthparents have described as "a psychological amputation." Therefore, the adoption intermediary has the responsibility, when approached, to understand the dynamics of an unplanned pregnancy. Assisting birthparents to explore all three options without placing value judgments on any one decision is the intermediary's duty and challenge.

Birthparents are capable of emotional maturation in confronting, coping, and growing with the unplanned pregnancy. This growth usually requires professional aid both in making an unhurried and informed decision, and then in accepting the chosen alternative. The adoption intermediary must have the skill, training, and time required to accomplish such professional counseling. Resource commitment for this process is costly. Therefore, the adoption intermediary might be tempted to accept a birthparent's initial approach and first decision. Counseling that points only to adoption certainly requires less time and energy. The end result of such narrow counseling also appears the same—an adoptive placement which makes two adoptive parents happy. The birthparents, however, may not be so happy. Once again, we emphasize that birthparents are not faceless, unfeeling baby machines who "will forget in time." Birthparents do not turn off their responsibility and love upon the signing of relinquishment papers.

The following two letters were written by one such birthmother, named Kristin. Her letters to her baby and the adoptive parents detail her experience with an unplanned pregnancy, delivery, and feelings after her baby's adoption:

Dear Beautiful People,
    I just found out today that you received my

baby. I don't know you and I don't know if our paths will ever cross in life, but I want you to know that I am eternally grateful to you, and I love you both with all my heart. It is really strange. We are so distant, but yet I feel so close to you, I know you people are gifts from God. My giving up this baby was the hardest thing in my life that I have ever done, but it was because I have loved her so much that I made my decision. I want her to have the kind of raising that I had, two loving parents that could provide her with the spiritual, emotional and material needs that are involved with raising a child. The main thing being <u>two parents</u> that love her, which is something I couldn't provide by myself. Don't get me wrong, I could smother her with love, but there is so much more to it than that that I know you can provide for her. I hope you don't mind me referring to her as "my" baby, I realize I gave her up legally, and she is yours, but I do have maternal feelings toward her. I hope you understand what I'm trying to say.

I'd like to share my life while pregnant and the delivery with you. I had no morning sickness with her, it was a perfect pregnancy, no problems whatsoever. I have always been "healthy" (plump—I don't like that word) so you couldn't really tell I was pregnant until about my seventh month. I just looked like I was gaining weight. I first felt her kick when I was about 5-1/2 months. It's really a neat feeling. As I got further along in the pregnancy, the harder she kicked. You could see it from the outside. If I placed both hands flat on my abdomen, I could feel her moving around At night I would usually sleep on my side, and she would sink to the side against the bed. When I got out of bed, I would have to check my balance because my lopsided stomach made me clumsy.

What else can I tell you—towards the end, she would sleep all day, and move around most of the night, much to my despair (ha ha). She was due on

January 11, but as you know was born January 24. That was the longest two weeks. To me it seemed longer than the whole pregnancy.

During the morning of January 23, I woke up with slight cramps, so I figured time was getting near. During the day they continued. They weren't painful, they felt like menstrual cramps. I didn't know what kind of pain to expect. I had always heard that the delivery is painful. As night came, the cramps started coming about every hour lasting about a minute or so. Gradually they came between 20 and 30 minutes apart. It was then I told the dorm mother, but I really wasn't sure because I didn't really hurt as I expected. I was calm throughout the time. I just kept waiting for bad pains but they never came. By midnight the cramps were 10-12 minutes apart, so the dorm mother said we would go to the hospital and let them check me just to made sure. So—we went and got there about 12:30.

The first thing the nurse asked me was if my water broke. When I said no, she said we didn't have to worry. They took me in the prep room and checked to see if I was dialated far enough yet. I measured at 6 cm. The nurse said she didn't believe I was that far along because I was so calm. It was at that time I started thinking "wow, this is really it." I asked how long they thought before the baby would be born and was told probably by 7:00 A.M. Well, they prepped me and my contractions were getting closer and starting to hurt—but still not like I expected. They put me in a room and gave me a shot for pain. I was supposed to be asleep for the delivery—I didn't want to remember it. Anyway, they measured me again. By this time it was about 1:15—I was 8 cm. I had a feeling it was going to be sooner than anticipated. A few minutes later they checked me again and said it was time to be wheeled into delivery. I was wondering when they were going to put me to sleep—I knew they couldn't do it too late. Then, the doctor walked in the room, and said it was too late, so I was awake throughout the entire thing. Now that I think about it, I'm glad I was awake, it all happened too fast. There was one real bad contraction and her head was born, then the rest of her just slid right out. She was laid upon my stomach for a few seconds—feeling her outside and inside is so different, it's such a separation. I remember her scream <u>loud</u> when the doctor slapped her—she has a healthy set of lungs. I was glad it was over, and I was ready to get back to my normal way of life.

The next day I went to see her, and got to hold her. I thought she was beautiful—I hope you do! It really hit me hard, the fact of what I was doing—as I was holding her, looking at her and thinking about her—I started crying. It hurt so much, but I knew what I wanted and what she needed. Even as young as I am, I realize that raising a child is a hard thing to do. There is happiness and there is pain, but you forget the pain because the happiness outweighs it. At this point, I really don't know what else to tell you—I'd like to keep in touch with you and you with me—but only if you want. I don't want you to feel I'm imposing, it's just that I'd like to know how your family is growing together. Also, I'd like to ask you to send me a picture of her in a few months—I'm curious to see what she looks like then, but I'm leaving the decision up to you. Whatever you feel best.

As you grow together in life, I imagine the baby when older will ask questions of her background. I don't know what you will tell her, but I know it will be the right thing. I'm writing her a letter also, and I want you to read it and give it to her when you feel that she is mature enough. If she decides that she wants to find me, please help her and don't feel threatened. I don't want to interfere with your relationship, and I won't do anything or say anything to hinder it. Remember, I love you too!

Well, I said most everything I wanted to so I'll

come to a close. If you have any questions— just let
me know, I'm keeping close contact with the
agency, and am looking forward to hearing from
you. God bless you and your family and may you
have a happy and prosperous life.

> Take care!
> I Love You
> Kristin

P.S. I kept this letter for a while trying to decide
whether I should add something or leave something out but decided this is what I really feel so I
chose to leave it as is.

Today Kristin is a nurse's aide and she looks forward to
finishing college, future marriage, and future children. Still,
her firstborn daughter is remembered, as much today as she
was when Kristin wrote her this letter:

My Daughter,
    I really don't know how to begin this letter.
There are so many things about you that I would
love to know. I imagine your main question is why.
I will try to explain that to you along with a few
other things from my life.
    I hope that by the time you read this, you are
old enough to understand my reasoning, and that
you don't hold it against me. I don't know what
your view on me will be because I'm not adopted. I
can only try to wonder what you are feeling. I want
you to know how grateful I am to your parents for
giving you a life that I couldn't. As I am writing this
letter I wonder at what time in your life you will
read this. I wonder what you look like, how old you
are, what your name is, and all kinds of things. I
guess the main thing I wonder about is if you ever
want to find me. I want to see you, but then I have
to think, I don't know how my life will be later. I
only hope the situation will permit it. There is one
thing I ask of you. If you do decide to come look for

me, please do it because you really want to find me, not for some unknown reason.

I'll tell you a bit about your biological background. First your father. He's tall, 6'2", thin, has black hair, beautiful brown eyes and he's very handsome. He's from Iran, born and raised there. He came to this county to go to college. He has five brothers and three sisters, and he's the baby of the family. He's 18 now. He's a very quiet person, also very serious. He was going to college for a degree in Chemical Engineering.

As for me, I'm 5'4", on the plump side (not thin for sure, but not really fat). I have brown hair, green eyes and I'm real light complected. I'm going to school for my R.N. and I have two more years to go. I have one brother, 6 years younger than me. I am 19. I want you to know your father was the first person I ever went to bed with. I felt in such a way for him that I hadn't felt for anyone else. We had a beautiful friendship at first and then it grew stronger. We had sex only one time, he never pressured or pushed me to it, it was by mutual agreement, and I didn't think one time would do any harm. That day was April 21. It was a few days before I was to leave college to go home. My parents never suspected my being pregnant. I knew it deep inside but I wouldn't admit it to myself. I just denied it. I hardly showed until I was 8 months pregnant. When I went back to school, I didn't tell your father. I knew he planned to go back to his country someday. Well as always, time went on. I had no plans as of what to do. Two of my best friends knew of my situation and they found the agency where I stayed until you were born. Baby, if you are anything like you were when I knew you—carried and delivered you—I know you are perfect. You never gave me a minute of trouble. Your delivery was perfect. I was awake and it wasn't painful—that much anyway. I don't imagine you know it, but we did have some time together. I watched you enter this big, wide world and I even got to hold you and feel you outside of me for a short time.

Your father didn't know anything about you until afterwards. I told him two months later. He was very hurt because he thought I was lying to him. At that time I knew I wouldn't see him again because he was going back home. I showed him my picture of you and he looked at it for a long time. I feel that in time he will accept the fact and I know that picture will remain in his mind forever. We parted that night with love and best wishes for both of us.

So many times now I feel lost. Love hurts very much, but life goes on and now I'm trying to carry on with my life. I date different guys, but I'm scared to get close to anyone. I don't want to lose them. I guess it will be this way for a while. I'm sure one day I will meet someone to take his place.

You know I think of you all the time. I see babies every day and wonder about you. I mentioned before that I got to hold you. You were beautiful—dark hair, light skin and bright blue eyes—oh yes and a beautiful nose. You were so trusting. As I held you I started crying. I loved and wanted you so much, but I had nothing. I had seen so many girls in my situation where it didn't work out, and I wanted you to have the best chance that life could give. I have memories of you that I will cherish forever. So babe, as you go along in life, be thankful you have the parents you do. They have given you everything that I couldn't. I brought you into the world, but they've done the hardest part—watching you grow, been with you in bad times as well as good, have helped you, have taken care of you, and done everything involved in leading a baby into a mature adult capable of living an adult life. One day in life, if it is God's will and destiny, we will meet again, if not we will live our lives to the fullest and carry on in a way we feel right for us. Just remember, any decision whether big or small will affect us in some way for all the days of our lives. So, baby, you take care of yourself. Do what your feel you need to do, and live your life the best way you can. Just be careful, life isn't always easy—but dwell on the good things. They outweigh the bad and remember I'll love you, and I'll never forget my first born baby.

Love always,
Kristin

P.S. I'm here if you need me—it's up to you.

Kristin's letters clearly illustrate the deep love birthparents have for their children. Adoptive placement does not erase those emotions. Adoption intermediaries can no longer ignore the reality and extent of these feelings by telling birthparents "you will or you should forget" (the third myth). The professional intermediary must provide the assistance required for birthparents to effectively resolve the crisis and consequences of an unplanned pregnancy.

PREGNANCY COUNSELING: THREE PHASES

The birthmother will go through three distinct phases in an unplanned pregnancy as we view it. The first phase spans the time from learning about the pregnancy to the birth of the child. The second phase begins with the birth of the baby. The third phase occurs after the child is placed in an adoptive home.

In this chapter, and frequently throughout the book, we write in terms of the birthmother rather than birthparents because regrettably the great majority of clients are birthmothers. Birthfathers, not undergoing physical changes, are capable of denying the reality of a pregnancy longer than most birthmothers. For that reason, we see fewer fathers. In addition, we have other access barriers to our birthfathers which account for our limited exposure to their unique needs. Nevertheless the birthfathers we have counseled have convinced us that the emotional experiences are the same for both parents—though they may differ in degree.

We strongly advocate that birthfathers not be forgotten. The adoption myth that sees the birthfather as "irresponsible and uncaring" is widely believed, making it easy for adoption intermediaries to overlook a birthfather's crisis. Without social support or counseling, the birthfather is likely to carry emotional scars as the aftermath of his child's placement. One birthfather told us (some fourteen years after his daughter was adopted) "I'll never have another child. It's the punishment I deserve for giving away my first."

Phase One—Before the Baby is Born

Fear, loneliness, and uncertainty permeate the initial phase of an unplanned pregnancy, lasting until the baby's birth. Counseling sessions in the beginning focus on the immediate crisis that led the birthmother to seek assistance. For some birthmothers this is dealing with how to tell their parents or other significant persons about their pregnancy. In other cases, the problem facing the birthmother is immediate financial need. In a few cases the initial crisis is overcoming a denial of the pregnancy and exploring the feelings that are hidden within the denial system. As we deal with these immediate factors birthmothers begin to examine their guilt about having made a mistake or having disappointed the people they love. Some of our clients at this point will select abortion as their alternative; and if that is their considered option, we assist them through proper referrals.

Once the immediate crisis is resolved, intensive counseling begins. Our goal is for the expectant mother to understand her pregnancy, herself, and the decision she will make. Through regular sessions we explore the options of keeping and of placing the child. She is assisted to consider the interests of each party based on the particular facts and circumstances of that client.

This requires the client to become educated about each alternative. We use various books on pregnancy and child development to explore child-raising issues. We encourage birthmothers to babysit or observe children of different age groups. We look past the baby stage to the child at two years, four years, and thirteen years in order to fully examine the birthmother's commitment to parenthood.

We also educate our clients about the realities of adoption, including the loss/grief experience and open adoption. We encourage birthparents to attend our monthly birthparents support group, where they meet with other birthparents who are at various stages in the process, including those in the post-adoption stage (sometimes several years post-birth). This gives them an opportunity to hear about the delivery/hospital experience, the grief experience, and the reality of ongoing contact. The adoption alternative, the feelings it awakens, and the personal consequences are all explored openly to reduce the confusion and isolation for the new birthmother.

Expectant birthparents also have an opportunity to meet and talk with adoptive parents. Laura, for example, attended an adoption workshop and talked about her reasons and plans to relinquish to prospective adoptive parents. She carefully and openly articulated her love for the child, and listened carefully to the story of another birthmother who relinquished two years earlier. Laura was tearful before attending the adoption workshop because it was her twenty-second birthday and she could not celebrate with her family due to her desire to keep her pregnancy a secret. In spite of her sadness, Laura decided to attend the adoption workshop. Afterwards, she reported feeling more confident about her decision as a result of her conversation with adoptive couples. Laura also later attended a special group session where three adoptive fathers spoke of their experiences in adopting.

Decision-making is not easy for our birthmothers. They frequently are sad and often vacillate in their plans. One technique we use is to ask birthmothers to keep an ongoing journal while in counseling and to list the advantages and disadvantages of each choice.

Through intensive professional counseling, women come to terms with their pregnancy and also the decision they will make. This process is similar to the process of coping with death. Birthmothers go through stages of denial, anger, sadness, and eventually acceptance. They need to work through each stage prior to delivery. The focus of the counseling is on the future of the unborn child as well as that of the birthmother.

We have found most pregnant women want to keep their babies. Decisions, however, must be based not on "wanting" or "wishing" but on what is best for the child, as well as what is best for the birthmother. Birthmothers we have counseled who have placed their babies for adoption could have adequately parented their children as single parents. They gave up their babies only because they believed this was in the best interest of the children and themselves. Placing a child for adoption is a considered and unselfish act of love.

Barbara was eighteen years old and planning to marry the birthfather of her baby when she found out she was pregnant. His parents, however, were so upset about the pregnancy that they pressured him to break off his relationship with her. Barbara felt betrayed and alone. She considered abortion, but couldn't bring herself to keep the appointment. Barbara entered a maternity group home, still confused about her plans for the future. This was a time of intense maturation. When she decided on adoption, she was eager for her child to be raised, as she was, in a rural community. Her letter to her son demonstrates her act of love through adoption:

Dear Little One,

First of all I want to tell you I love you more than anything in this world. I don't want you to feel badly towards me because I gave you up. The reason is because I love you. I could not have supported you and given you everything I wanted you to have. I loved your father very much or so I thought. He had his own life to live and apparently you and I were not to be a part of it. I'm sure he loves you in his own way but we must have been meant to go our separate ways. You now have <u>two</u> parents who are very wonderful and very beautiful people who could not love you anymore than they do now. One day if you feel the need to find me for any reason I'll be here. But do not expect anything from me except love. I gave up my rights to you a long time ago and I accept that and I hope that you will also. The parents you have now are your real

parents. They've taken care of your every need
since you were only a few days old. I am the one
who gave birth to you but I couldn't give you anything more, and I can give nothing now except my
love. All I ask of you is to love your parents and live
a good life. I pray you reach all your goals and have
a happy and fulfilled life. I love you.

> May God Bless You
> and Keep You Always,
> Your Birthmother

An important task during this stage is selecting the adoptive
parents. If the birthmother feels definite about adoption, she
may make this decision early in her pregnancy and early in
the counseling process in order to establish a close relationship with the adoptive parents during the duration of the pregnancy. In other situations, the birthmother may participate in
several counseling sessions before deciding on adoption and
selecting the adoptive parents.

In many adoption agencies, the social workers select
several couples to suggest to the birthmother. They provide
the birthparents with profiles written by the social workers or
letters written by the couples to enable the birthparents to
make their selection. In other adoption programs (where
clients are in control of their own adoption) the birthparents
select the adoptive parents from *all* adoptive parents available—there is no pre-selection or "screening" by third parties.
Instead, that is the role and responsibility of the birthparents.
Prospective adoptive parents write "Birthmother Letters" in
order to introduce themselves to the birthparents and to share
their interest/hopes/dreams in looking forward to parenthood.

This is an example of a "Birthmother Letter" (which
adoption intermediaries keep on file to show birthparents and
which adoptive couples also distribute to friends and con-
tacts in the hopes of locating a potential birthmother):

Hi,

Oh, how we have always dreamed of parenthood
one day, and as yet we have not been able to realize

that dream. We dreamed of making our child's first Halloween costume and taking them trick-or-treating to their grandparent's house to surprise them, watching their little faces on Christmas Day with a surprise visit from Santa Claus himself, and then our annual family reunion picnic. Coming from large Italian families, all these holidays are happily celebrated. What has meant a lot to us is that, between both of us, we are godparents to 8 children, which happens to be some of our best friend's children. Larry is the best diaper changer and Darlene enjoys going to the park and feeding the ducks, things we long to do with a child of our own. Reading bedtime stories, playing peek-a-boo, holding our baby and doing a lot of kissing are part of our dream.

For 15 years we have tried to have a family of our own. We were advised to see an infertility specialist as Darlene wasn't able to conceive and she still did not get pregnant. Both our parents have been very supportive throughout these hard times, but they were thrilled at Thanksgiving time to find out that we were planning to adopt. They are already planning to buy baby clothes and toys.

Our country style home borders Mt. Diablo State Park in the town of Danville in Northern California. Our backyard is spacious enough for swings and jungle gyms. Our dog Andy, an all white fluffy Lhasa Apso, loves to romp and run throughout the yard. Living next door to a State Park has its advantages as Mother Nature is all around us: rolling green hills to tumble down, over 100 year old oak trees to climb, and a lot of deer.

Larry is a businessman operating a five store retail delicatessen manufacturing and importing business. Darlene has just resigned her position as a Customer Relations Supervisor to devote her time to see this adoption through and is excited about finally becoming a full time Mom.

We both love to travel, attend stage plays, symphonies, and do a lot of walking. Larry can't wait to travel to Grandma and Grandpa's cabin in the Sierra Mountains to show our child the snow for the first time. Darlene imagines a little one helping her make chocolate chip cookies (and eating all the chocolate chips), or licking the spatula and getting cake batter all over their little face with sticky fingers tugging at her apron.

If you would like to talk to us about adopting your child, please call us collect at _____ or call our Adoption Advisors at the Independent Adoption Center at (800) 877-OPEN.

In Friendship,
Larry & Darlene Cerletti

Phase Two—The Birth Experience

The second phase of an unplanned pregnancy begins with the child's birth. Although most birthmothers reach a preliminary decision before their child is born, the actual birth of their baby necessitates a reevaluation of that decision. The reality of a child evokes new emotions that must be examined. Regrettably, adoption intermediaries often encourage the birthmother, at this point, to accept the decision which she had been leaning toward without reassessing her alternatives. These intermediaries tend to focus more on the product (a child available for adoptive placement) than on the birthmother's emotional needs. Arrival of the baby, however, is a very critical stage of the unplanned pregnancy for the birthmother. If she is to accept her decision for a lifetime, post-delivery support and counseling must not be hasty or ignored.

In the hospital, we encourage the birthmother to look at her current feelings toward her baby and adoption. We also encourage all birthmothers to see, hold, and feed the child. In part, this contact with the baby reinforces the birthmother's feelings of self-worth by learning she could manage a baby if she elected to parent the child. In addition, it is important for her to bond with the baby before she can separate from him—one must say "hello" before one can say "good-bye."

During this time she can also explain to the baby why she has made an adoption decision.

In addition, contact with the child prevents any denial. The first stage of grieving is denial, and we want our birthmothers to move past that stage before they place the baby for adoption. We want our birthmothers to decide to place their child *only after coming to terms with that child's reality.* Crystal, a young birthmother, recalls, "I was afraid that when I saw the baby I was not going to be able to go through with the adoption, but I had to see him. I had too much curiosity. Right when I saw him I knew I couldn't keep him. I knew it would be wrong. I knew I couldn't be so selfish."

Decisions made in the post-delivery phase may be complicated by family and peer pressures. For example, we sometimes see birthgrandparents become strongly attached to their grandchild. This leads them to pressure their daughter to keep her newborn baby, usually ignoring her own desires. Intermediary support for the birthmother is once again necessary so that she may make her own decision in the face of outside pressures.

Mindy was nineteen when she discovered she was pregnant. Marriage was not a realistic alternative, so Mindy seriously considered single parenthood. She had the complete support of her parents for whatever decision she made. In fact, her parents came to visit her and the baby in the hospital and became very attached to their first grandchild. Mindy frequently fed and held her baby in the hospital and she named him Marshall. But Mindy had strong feelings about wanting her baby to have a two-parent family and she didn't feel able to handle the responsibility of single parenthood. She chose adoption and wrote the following letter to Marshall's new family:

Dear Family,

Everytime I try to start this letter I get stuck. I really don't know what to say to you I know you will be good parents and take good care of my son and love him as your very own. That makes me feel good and very happy. My parents are also glad to know he will be well taken care of. My mother loved him very much because he was her first grandchild. It was very hard for her as well as for me to give him up. He is a very special little boy to us.

I will ask a few things of you. Please help guide him toward what he would like to be but please don't pressure him. And please let him know about me and help him to understand that I didn't give him up because I didn't want him or because something was wrong with him.

I would definitely like to meet him and your family someday. I will in no way try to win him back. I just want to let him know in person that I love him.

Your Son's Birthmother

In some states, legal relinquishment papers may be signed by birthmothers ready for that decision while still in the hospital. In other states, the relinquishment/consent is signed at some later date (typically the time period is dictated by state laws).

In all cases, we recommend that the baby be placed directly from the hospital with the adopting parents, rather than utilizing foster care. This means that in cases where the birthparents have not yet signed the relinquishment, the adoptive parents must be willing to take some legal risk. This enables the adoptive family and baby to bond with one another from the beginning, and it also minimizes the separations and adjustments for the infant.

Phase Three—Living with the Adoption Decision

The final phase of the unplanned pregnancy begins for the birthmother after the child is placed in the adoptive home. The post-birth period is the time the birthmother both grieves and begins the process of accepting her decision. We now understand that counseling at this stage is essentially grief counseling. One birthmother who placed her child for adoption ten years ago recalls that her agency provided no post-placement guidance. She relates painfully, "No one told me that I would experience overpowering feelings of grief. I was totally unprepared for the emotions that hit me." This same birthmother also lacked understanding family members or friends to assist her through the painful days and nights of missing her child. The professional intermediaries who should have been with her were either rationalizing that she did not care about her birthchild (first myth of adoption) or that she had forgotten by now (third myth).

In contrast, we acknowledge the feelings of grief felt by birthparents by preparing them prior to delivery and by providing post-placement grief counseling. Counseling begins on the day of the child's adoptive placement (typically at discharge from the hospital), which marks the start of the child's existence separate from his birthmother. Our involvement then continues as long as the birthparent feels our support is necessary.

Since our birthmothers select the adoptive parents of their child, they feel a special love for the adoptive parents. They know that placement day is a day of joy for the people they picked to parent their child. This helps ease some of their own sadness. In fact, birthparents with open adoptions work through the normal feelings of loss and grief much more quickly and easily because they have selected the parents for their baby, have met with them, and will continue to have contact with them over the years. This gives them a peace of mind not found in closed adoption and enables them to more easily deal with their grief.

Letters, pictures, and gifts are frequently exchanged between birthparents and adoptive parents during the post-birth period (and, in open adoptions, there are also visits). Hal and Marcie, an adoptive couple, wrote two letters to the birthmother of their son. The first letter was written one month after placement and the second one seven months later. Both were eagerly received by a birthmother working to integrate and accept her act of placing a child:

> To our son's biological mother,
>   It is impossible to describe the joy of being presented with such a beautiful child. We had wanted a child for a long time and had tried very hard to have our own. Now we are sure that adopting your

biological son was what God meant for us. He has brought us so much happiness—we could never have asked for a more perfect child.

When we went to pick him up that day, we were nervous wondering what he would look like and how we would feel about him. But when we saw him, all the nervousness went away. He was more that we had ever imagined. We have loved him from that moment, and every day we can feel the love grow.

We feel, as you do, that he deserves every chance to enjoy life. Being good parents to him is very important to us, and we promise to do everything we can to help him have a happy and fulfilling life. We will help him to develop and grow and give him every opportunity to get the most possible out of life.

We want you to know that you are very special to us, too. We know that releasing your child was difficult, and we want to assure you that he will always be very much loved by us. We wish you the best, and while we know you will never forget your biological son, we hope that when you think of him it will be with happiness and good feelings. That is also how we want him to feel about you. It's so little for us just to say thanks—but thank you very much. God bless you always, and may He give you all the love and happiness the world has to offer.

Love, Your biological son's parents

To our son's birthmother,

Hi! I heard from our social worker today, and she said you would like to have a picture of the baby. We are sending one when he was about five months old; we hope you like it.

We think about you a lot and hope everything is going okay for you. We are all doing really fine and are enjoying our new little family member so much.

He's eight months old now—it's hard to

believe he's been with us that long. He's still a very happy and content little boy. He has been healthy and made it through the winter without anything serious. He has five teeth and is starting to eat some table foods which he loves. He's also learning to drink from a cup. He has been crawling for about a month and can pull himself to a standing position and walk along a sofa or table by himself. I think he will walk for sure within a month. He does "pat-a-cakes" when we say the words for him and has also started making some really silly noises with his hand in his mouth. He likes to pull hair, including his own, which still looks like it's going to be blonde. He has beautiful blue eyes and the sweetest little smile. He loves people—we think it's really nice because he's not shy or afraid of other people. He gets all excited when he's around other babies especially. I think he's going to be very outgoing and friendly. He still loves his bath. When he gets in the tub he swims and splashes and squeals with excitement. We can't wait until it gets warmer so we can get him a little splash pool to play in. He also has a puppy that he likes. The puppy usually stays outside, so he crawls over to the window to visit with it. When we put him outside in his swing sometimes, the puppy licks his toes, and they both think that's funny. He's still very curious and observant. We never have trouble if we take him anywhere (to the grocery store, mall, restaurant etc.) because he's so busy looking at everything that he doesn't get fussy.

So we are really happy with the way everything has worked out. We hope to be able to adopt another baby in a couple of years. I think I told you before how sad and depressed I used to be when I kept trying and trying and could never get pregnant. I used to pray and wonder why it could happen to other people and not me. Since we have had this baby with us, I have never again wondered why I never got pregnant. There is no doubt in my mind that God, in His way, was saving us to be the parents of this wonderful little boy. I hope you feel as good about it as we do.

Please take care of yourself, and God be with you always. I love you and feel close to you even though I really don't know you And please feel assured that your biological son is very much loved and cared for.

Love,
Your birthson's mother

Sylvia, the birthmother who received these letters told us "When I think of him, I think of him being with his puppy dog or in the bath. I just think of him as being happy." She adds, "In a way I was a chosen person to have this baby for someone else who couldn't." Today she describes adoption as "giving love all the way around."

At this early post-placement phase, correspondence and pictures of the baby from the adoptive parents assure the birthmother that her child is developing and happy. In turn, the birthmother can assure the adoptive parents of their place in the child's life. Polly, an eighteen-year-old birthmother, wrote the following letter to her daughter's parents shortly after the placement:

Dear Adoptive Parents,

I hope you are enjoying your daughter. I know she will be happy there with you, and I hope you love her as much as I do. I'm glad she has a loving family such as yours. It gives me a great feeling of security to know she has parents like you and a big brother.

I can imagine how much you have wanted this child, and I thank you so much for giving her what I could not. I can not begin to express my feelings of gratitude.

I hope everything is going well at your home, and I wish you the best always.

Take care,
Polly

The post-birth stage also involves "reentering the world" and establishing new relationships. The birthmother must decide "whom do I tell," and how to respond if someone says, "How could you do that?" Birthmothers often worry about dating again and some must come to terms with anger directed at males in general. In addition, family adjustments can be awkward since families tend to deny that the pregnancy occurred.

To deal with these post-adoption issues, we provide both individual counseling and a monthly birthparents support group. The group consists of other birthmothers who have placed their children for adoption and are in the process of both accepting their decisions and rebuilding their lives. Discussions center on such topics as sex, birth control, family interaction, assertiveness training, and ongoing contact with the adoptive parents and child. Often our birthmothers feel "no one else fully understands," and the group becomes their opportunity to talk about the child and themselves. Attendance is usually regular during the first few months and then sporadic. The group provides essential social support and information necessary to get through this final phase of the unplanned pregnancy. Each birthmother progresses through the stages of grief at her own pace.

Sandra, age nineteen, attended our support group sessions regularly for an entire year. It took Sandra that much time before she was finally able to say goodbye in this letter.

Dear Daughter,

I am writing this letter almost one year after I had you because I feel like it is something that I must do before too long. I want you to know my reasons for giving you up and tell you that you are now and will be forever in my thoughts. There were many times that I would change my mind but in the end my decision was the best for everyone all the way around. I want you to know that if your birthfather and I could have provided for you everything necessary, we would have done so. When I say provided for you, I mean everything needed to raise a child including love for each other, which was not there. I don't think I was old enough to take the responsibility of raising a child either. I am sure that if your birthfather and I loved each other as much as we love you we could have done it. However, it wasn't that way between us. We thought we did, but when it came to talking about the rest of our lives, I really don't think it was there. I am sure now that you are happy and have the most wonderful parents ever dreamed of. They are warm, loving people and I admire them very much. I know you will grow into a beautiful person and have a great life. I cannot put down into writing the way I feel about you. Now that a year has passed by, my life has gone on and the memories that I have of you are stored in a special place in my heart. Your birthfather and I have remained friends and we both hope that we may see you someday. I hope your feelings will be the same and your can understand our reasons for placing you for adoption.

Love always,
Your Birthmother

P.S. I also want you to know that you were the biggest baby in the hospital nursery and surely the healthiest. Good luck always.

DECIDING ABOUT FUTURE CONTACT

In agency adoption, the birthmother typically makes one final decision before she terminates her relationship with the agency. She must answer the question: "Do you want future contact from your child?" The birthmother signs a document about whether she wants records opened if her child later (at age 18 or older) decides to search. In our experience, 99% of birthmothers consent to future contact. In some agencies, birthmothers also are invited to participate in exchanging ongoing correspondence and current pictures with their adoptive parents, but typically the agency remains the intermediary for this contact. Most birthmothers are positive about both opportunities.

In fully open adoption birthparents and adoptive parents share full identifying information from the beginning and have access to direct ongoing contact over the years. The "open records at age 18" issue is not relevant, because these individuals remain in contact over the years, and the adoptive parents can easily put the adopted child/adult in direct contact with his birthmother.

Each birthparent ends her relationship with the adoption intermediary when she is ready, and always with the assurance that she may contact us for information or assistance at any future time. We know her decision was a lifetime one; therefore, we plan to meet her needs as time and the healing process demands, even if it takes that lifetime.

Ultimately we find that our parents—both birth and adoptive—provide most of the long-term support for each other. Any communication is usually welcomed by all parties. Pam, the birthmother who wrote the following letter, thought she had lost this special relationship when she stopped hearing from Raymond and Debbie, the adoptive parents of her daughter. The adoptive parents had written but their letter had disappeared somehow in the mail:

> Dear Raymond and Debbie,
>
> I was so relieved to hear from the agency that I just couldn't wait to write you a letter. The reason I haven't written is because I felt that it would be in vain. The last letters I wrote were in the beginning of February. I got no response and I was <u>very</u> worried and upset. I thought you folks just didn't want to write, so I've left you alone. It's good to know that you <u>do</u> want to hear from me.
>
> Things have changed quite a bit for me! I've got a job at a bank downtown here as a teller. It's a good job except for the pay. In November the bank financed a car for me. It's real nice! It's a little Plymouth Arrow. I haven't got my own place yet, but I'm working on it. It won't be long. Best of all, I have a boyfriend who I love very much. He's a

good person. One thing I know is that he loves children. I've told him about Brenda and all of you. He thinks it's wonderful to have adoptive parents who care enough to try to keep in touch. I do too. If possible, it would be nice to have some more pictures of Brenda. I'm dying to know how she's doing and what's going on in her life. I'm sure she's just as beautiful as I imagine. I enclosed a picture of myself. I don't look very happy 'cause the sun was in my eyes. I'll have to send a better one when I have them done in a portrait studio. That's me, anyway (pudgy). I only want to say one thing about her birthfather. He cares more about Brenda than he does about himself. That's enough about me, except that I hope to have another child whose as beautiful as Brenda. I can't wait to find out what's going on there with all of you (including Brad). I'd love to hear from you.

> Joyfully,
> Pam

Pam's letter is "joyous" because she is allowed open communication to people who have a permanent place in her thoughts. The depth of the bond that can form between our "collective parents" is truly unique. The next letter written by Dawn two years after her son's adoptive placement reveals just how and why the bond is so special:

Dearest Terry, Nancy, and Drew,
Thank you so very much for those wonderful pictures. Drew is such a beautiful boy. I am so proud of him. I have been keeping all of Drew's pictures in my photo-album with the exception of two that I carry with me. Since you sent a picture of you both, I now added those pictures to my album. As I was putting the pictures in the photo book, I thought to myself "now I have my family all together," and that is how I feel. You are a very special and important part of my life. You, Terry and Nancy, have a special place in my heart. Drew holds

a special (very special) spot all his own, and no one but no one will ever take that love for you three away from me. I just want you to know that I have a big, big heart that holds lots, lots of love. So much love that I will never be able to express all the love I have for Drew and the both of you. I do know one thing, that love grows and grows each day. More and more as I look at Drew's pictures and more and more as I read your letters. I hope and pray that we will be able to continue writing and exchanging pictures. I also was curious and excited when I received your pictures. Nancy, you have very pretty eyes and such a kind friendly smile. Terry you're very handsome. I know you are tall, but boy, you have large hands. I bet you'd make a good football player or basketball, too.

I don't think I would feel the same toward you two, if it wasn't for your letters. Knowing and being showed that you do care for me and you really, really do care and love our son Drew, has lifted a heavy load off my shoulders.

Sure, I wish I would of had a good home for our son and a father, cause I would never of put Drew up for adoption. But that was just it—I didn't have the surroundings and environment to bring up a child. I feel that it would of been selfish to of tried to raise Drew by myself. At the time I was all alone. It was just me. I used to cry and cry before Drew was born. What was I to do! Oh, I tell you I lived in a nightmare. I tried to hide the fact that I was pregnant from my friends and family. (My good old boyfriend left me.) It was just me and Drew. I had no one to turn to, talk to. I used to sit down and tell all my problems to a big white stuffed rabbit I have. That old rabbit knows me better than anyone.

Then I thought to myself, my baby (at that time, now he's ours) is going to have the best, and that's when I made my mind to relinquish my baby. It was at that moment I hurt. I didn't know where

Drew would go, who would be raising him. I had all
these questions, these thoughts running through
my head, one after another. When Drew was born
(which was the greatest experience in my life) and
they hit me with those papers (adoption relinquishment papers) I felt confused and hurt, my life
was gone, down the drain. It wasn't until I received
three pictures of Drew and a letter from my social
worker that I felt a little less guilt. Then when I
received your letter that was handwritten by you to
me, that the guilt, the sorrow, the confusion went
away. I knew Drew was where he belonged and
belongs. You know that saying, time heals all—well
it heals, but the past —at least for me—will always
be remembered. I was also told the old saying! "Out
of sight, out of mind"—not so. I think about Drew
and you both all the time.

I wonder at times what it would be like to give
Drew a hug and kiss, to hold him, to play with him,
but then I realize that you do that for me. I wouldn't
want Drew with any other parents. You are the
best. I can tell by all of Drew's pictures he is so
happy and healthy looking.

I wish for a day where I'll be able to come to
you, Terry and Nancy, and tell you how much I love
you and all the gratitude I have for you. I wish for
a day where I'll be able to confront Drew about our
situation. I hope Drew and I will someday meet and
become friends. I know I will never be his mother.
I don't want that. You are the only parents that
he'll grow to love and know. But I want to be able
to talk to my family face to face because there is so
much love and feelings toward you that I just can't
put down on paper. I know God created Drew
through me for you, but God also created you for
Drew and me!

It made me feel so good when you said Drew
looks like me. I agree. My mother and I got out
some baby pictures of me and compared them with
Drew's. We came to the conclusion Drew has my

nose, my smile, hair and shape of face. He got his big blue eyes from his father—Sam as I think I mentioned in a previous letter. . . .

I have 4 months of school left until I graduate. I am really excited about my career and future. I'm looking forward to getting settled into a job. Most of all I'm looking forward to getting married in July or August, and within 3 years (give or take a year), starting a family of my own. I know God will let Jim and I know when that time will be. God sure blessed us with a beautiful son, Drew, and God blessed Drew with you.

God Bless You and Keep You,
All My Love
Dawn

Dawn's letter is open and secure. She can write of her pain and of her hopes for her future to the adoptive parents of her son. Her healthy adjustment is the result of careful professional counseling. The task is not simple—adoption intermediaries must commit time, personnel, and other resources necessary. But to do less would be a disservice to those birthparents who select adoption as their best alternative.

8
Adoption—
A New Definition

Legacy of an Adopted Child

Once there were two women
Who never knew each other
One you do not remember
The other you call mother

Two different lives shaped to make yours one
One became your guiding star
The other became your sun

The first gave you life
And the second taught you to live in
The first gave you a need for love
And the second was there to give it

One gave you a nationality
The other gave you a name
One gave you the seed of talent
The other gave you an aim

One gave you emotions
The other calmed your fears
One saw your first sweet smile
The other dried your tears

One gave you up—it was all that she could do.
The other prayed for a child.
And God led her straight to you.

And now you ask me through your tears,
The age old questions through the years;

Heredity or Environment—which are you
    the product of:

Neither my darling—neither
    Just two different kinds of love.
                        Anonymous

We have identified the myths of adoption and explored how new adoption practices affect adoptive parents and birthparents. In this chapter, we propose a new definition of adoption. This definition is offered primarily for the last member of the adoption drama—the adoptee.

Our definition of adoption is a simple statement, but contains no simple concepts:

Adoption is the process of accepting the responsibility of raising an individual who has two sets of parents.

To understand what this definition conveys we will examine first what we term the grammar of adoption and then the precise words of two phrases within our definition. Why the emphasis on "responsibility?" What are the consequences of the ending phrase "an individual who has two sets of parents?"

THE GRAMMAR OF ADOPTION

We began our definition with the phrase "adoption is the process." When couples elect to adopt, they think and talk in terms of adoption being the process necessary to form their family. Emphasis is on the act or event of adoption. Such statements as the following are typical: "We have started the adoption process," or "The agency will place a child with us next week." In a sense, adoption is being used here to describe a single event which will form their family.

In contrast, once the couple does adopt a child, a semantic problem develops. Parents who want to share with another that their child was adopted stumble with such statements as: "Betsy is my adopted daughter;" "I have two special children and one natural child;" "I have one chosen child and one of my own;" or "I only have one biological child." In each instance, the terms they use to convey an "adoptive status" are applied as adjectives to describe the child. The dictionary defines an adjective as "denoting a quality of the thing named." By applying "adopted" or "special" or "chosen" or "biological" to the child, it sounds as if there are different kinds of children (as represented by adjectives) instead of different ways for children to enter a family (as represented by a process).

Adoption is a process. We advocate that the process be kept distinct from the person who is the adoptee. On the simplest level this means preferring "Betsy was adopted" to "Betsy is an adopted child." The first (Betsy was adopted) correctly describes a single and past event in her life. This is no different from a birthmother proud of the experience of giving birth describing to another, "I had my son by cesarean birth." The same birthmother would not refer to that child after the event as "my cesarean son."

By contrast, "Betsy is an adopted child" or even "Betsy is special because she is adopted" conveys an ongoing significance to the state of being adopted. This is potentially dangerous because of the subtle implication that adopted children are somehow different from natural children who do not have labels attached to them. In addition, if Betsy is described as "special" or "chosen," that means someone is less special or valuable as a person. If Betsy is not a "natural child" that makes her "unnatural" or at least not normal. Do these labels all mean that at one point Betsy was not so special because she was not wanted?

The goal of our definition is more than a careful selection of the "right word." Being clear that adoption is a process recognizes that there are different ways to create a family, but the children of that family are not different. When speaking in terms of the way the family was formed, the preferable approach is, "Betsy was adopted." When talking about Betsy herself, she is simply "our daughter." Emphasis remains where it belongs.

Frank and Ellen, an adoptive couple who waited for several years for their son, enjoy describing their adoption experience and do so with pride. Note that when they want to talk about the adoption they use such phrases as, "manner he entered our family." When they speak of their son, the terminology is simply "our precious little son," without qualifying adjectives:

> To The Birth-Mother of Our Son:
>
> Somehow writing this letter is much harder than we could have ever anticipated. There are so many feelings inside of us it's really difficult to put them down on paper. There are no words to tell you how grateful we are to be the proud new parents of a darling little son. He is definitely God's gift to us in life. It's positively a dream come true. One day we were just an ordinary couple who had wanted children for many years and then suddenly we are blessed with one of God's most dearest gifts—a baby boy! There is nothing on this earth more precious to us than our little son!
>
> In the future we will be impressing upon him the importance of life and a close family relationship. We don't feel that the manner in which he entered our family is of any importance at all. The important thing is that he's ours for keeps now and that's what really counts.
>
> Please know that we will tell him everything we know about where he came from. We want him to grow up knowing his natural parents did what was best for him at the time. We hope he will think of the whole situation with understanding and compassion. It sincerely touches our hearts to know that some women care enough about their child to give him up knowing he will be placed in a loving, happy home.
>
> We believe that it is God's will that we can't have children naturally. But we now know that God has a plan for each of us and for months when we were sure he'd forgotten about us and we'd even doubted him, he came through and showed us that he had other more important plans for us. Now our lives have taken on a whole new meaning.

We know this must be a very difficult time for you. We think about you many times during the course of a week. We wonder how you have adjusted and if you will ever want him to look you up. We were told that you were also adopted. This being the case we hope you will want to share any information you may obtain about your natural parents so that he will be able to have answers to his many questions.

We want to help our son to obtain any goal he should set for himself. If he should decide that he'd like to meet you some day—well, we're all for it. That is, of course, if it is also what you want. We would not want to invade your privacy or interrupt your life in any way unless you say it is alright.

We do not feel threatened by you nor do we feel like his meeting you will change the way we feel about each other. We love each other very much and we will have been with him through good times and bad and so whatever he decides is also our decision.

Our hearts will always hold a special place for you and we will pray that God will give you the strength to accept what has happened to you and know that someday you will realize that you made the right decision and find out what God's plans for your life will be. Sometimes when you least expect it, there comes a miracle from God to set your life back on track.

Many thanks to you! We know that what you did was only for yourself and the love of a little one but that decision has affected our lives greatly too.

May God Bless You and Keep You Forever and Ever and may we say "Thank You" for allowing this little boy to come into the world and bless our lives.

Gratefully yours,
Baby's New Parents

Adoptive parents often tend initially to glamorize adoption with the terms "special" or "chosen" in order to convey the experiences and emotion they have invested in the process. Their initial tendency is also a protective counter to bolster their status, in case others equate an infrequently used process to a second best one. The definition we promote assists our parents to recognize that the process of giving birth and the process of adoption result in the same objective—a family. Once that family is formed the procedure is over and should become a fact in the family's life history, as any other past event. Although the act of adopting is not the most frequent way Americans form their families, the relationship so formed is just as complete. Again, distinguishing the procedure from the family so formed prevents subtle messages or thoughts that the family is less valuable or second best to the family formed through the birth process.

ACCEPTING RESPONSIBILITY

Adoption is the process of **accepting the responsibility** of raising an individual who has two sets of parents.

When adoptive parents accept a child into their family they acquire some unique parental obligations. Adoptive parents are accountable for telling their child he was adopted, and for sharing adoption information in a natural and honest manner. This allows the adoptee to integrate simple and straightforward facts into his evolving identity.

We still hear that in some cases adoptive parents have waited to share the fact of their child's adoption until the child "could understand." This approach anticipates a "right time," but contains many hazards. The most dramatic danger, of course, is when the "right time" does not occur when the child could first understand, because the adoptive parents keep "forgetting." Finally, the adoptee is told, possibly at the same time he is coping with the identity-seeking teen years. The shock of such a revelation at this time can be very destructive. The adoptee can understandably react as if his entire life has been a lie. He may even believe that he no longer has a foundation upon which to base his value system. Trust in the family unit can be forever shattered. Although this scenario still occurs, such a blow to the adoptee's identity and security is unnecessary.

More subtle hazards of waiting to share adoption information until the adoptee can understand include overemphasizing the significance of his adoption. Waiting usually means that the telling includes an elaborately staged family conference called to convey an important message. This creates an atmosphere that says adoption is so different we treat the subject (and you?) as out of the ordinary.

Another danger of waiting until the "right time" is that the unveiling occurs at a period in time when the adoptee is not interested. Because he does not ask questions and shows no other interest at this initial family session, his parents assume he both understands and is satisfied with the information they did share. Parents might even be tempted to seek the solace of this rationalized conclusion because of their own need not to remember or talk about his adoption. Often these parents are surprised and saddened by future probing questions from the same adoptee. Their answers at this point reflect these feelings of surprise, sadness, and some anger. Adoptees quickly pick up on their parents' feelings. Recently Adam, an adult adoptee speaking at a group meeting remembered, "For every question I was able to ask my parents, I had a thousand more." He never asked those additional questions because he was sensitive to the distress the inquiry would cause his parents.

To counter these hazards, we advocate a gradual and natural approach that keeps the responsibility always on the adoptive parents. We refer to our method as a building block process and it begins when the child is an infant (assuming an early placement). We advocate this early approach because of the fact that children learn to talk by imitating words they hear. If they hear "adoption" in the home, they will learn to use the word even before they fully understand its meaning. Many of our two-year-olds tell people, "I 'dopted"with the same understanding as when they hold up two fingers in response to questions of age. As adults, these adoptees will not recall their first introduction to adoption. The term and the subject will be naturally accepted. To assure the adoptee this type of introduction, adoptive parents have the responsibility of using the word "adoption" freely in the home during their family's initial bonding period. This is difficult for parents to do during the early adoptive period because many work to deny the realities of adoption. To safeguard the adoptee's future attitudes toward himself, adoption, and his parents, we strongly recommend that this first building block be provided.

Between two and five years of age, the child's next building block is offered by the adoptive parents. The objective is for the adoptee to associate the word adoption with the formation of his family. A second goal is to accomplish this familiarization in a relaxed manner aimed at his level of understanding. This can be done by reading or telling the adoptee stories of adoption. Homemade picture scrapbooks of the child or such books as Carole Livingston's *Why Was I Adopted* (1978) work very well. Such a presentation, combined with the previous free use of the word, lays a foundation for the adoptee to accept his adoption in much the same way he accepts his eye or hair color. That is, no value judgments are placed on the adoption process. He sees it as neither good nor bad.

Remember adoption is a process—a process that does not describe the adoptee as an individual. That concept, however, would be difficult to explain to a four-year-old. Therefore, the manner we convey adoption facts should be calculated to nonverbally express our attitude. We recommend a storybook approach because the preschooler loves books. We also find the storybook setting creates an informal atmosphere while giving adoptive parents the instructional support of visual aides.

Subsequent building blocks are added as the curiosity of the child and ingenuity of the parents dictate. School age children begin to ask in-depth questions about their heritage and about the two individuals who are their birthparents. This begins the period when adoptive parents must deal with their own feelings in response to the adoptee's questions. This is especially true when the child uses such phrases as "my other mother" or "my real father." Although we acknowledge their own emotional needs, adoptive parents have the crucial task during these years of keeping communication channels open. Their objective is to create a comfortable atmosphere that says, "your questions are welcomed and will be answered."

In order to convey honest facts to the adoptee, adoptive parents must know and understand birthparents. This includes fully exploring the myths of adoption and their own particular stereotypes. We assist our adoptive parents with this exploration and with their own emotional growth. We are convinced adoptive parents can comfortably share accurate adoption information once they have resolved any ambivalence toward their child's birthparents.

The following letter was written by an adoptive mother to the birthmother of her son more than three years after the adoption. The letter reflects security in her own role and in the role the birthmother plays in Cliff's life. They will be able to communicate with their son about his birthparents without sadness, envy, or threat. We know Cliff is only one of the several beneficiaries:

> Dear Dee,
>
> We have read your letters and looked at your pictures so many times. I'm sorry that it has taken me so long to write, but it's been hard to think of what to say.
>
> We have appreciated, cherished and saved your letters and poems for Cliff. I know they will be very important to him to know how much you care and your feelings. Your letters have helped reassure us, and eased our fears.
>
> Cliff is the light in our lives. He is growing so much everyday. It's amazing how quickly he changes. I'm enclosing a recent picture. He looks like he has your coloring, and your pictures will mean so much to him.
>
> It really sounds like school and your job have kept you busy. I hope your music is recorded, too. My brother is very musical. He writes and plays his own music as a hobby.
>
> We have gotten brave and are trying to adopt another baby. We are waiting and when we ask Cliff what he wants he says "I want a BIG baby!"

Thank you for your letters and thoughtfulness. I hope things continue to go well for you, because you are someone who has an important place in our hearts.

Yours Truly,
Jill and Mike

As the child matures, further additional details of his adoption will unfold. During this time, adoptive parents must carefully balance the desire to allow the adoptee to explore the topic at his own pace against the peril of the subject becoming a closed one in the home. An unhealthy closure might easily occur if adoptive parents assume that silence means no interest. Adoptees tell us a different story. Again, we emphasize that adoptive parents (not the child) have the responsibility to periodically bring up the subject. This is done either to explore possible areas of concerns or to merely reassure the adoptee that the subject is not taboo.

These responsibilities are unique. Adoptive parents provide more than the moral, legal, and nurturing aspects of parenthood. They prepare their child to face life with an open, informed, and relaxed acceptance of the fact that he was adopted. Such responsibility might appear awesome but our adoptive parents, like the following adoptive father, gladly accept the task:

Dear Friend,

I'm sorry I have not written to you before now. You have been on my mind many times since my wife and I received your baby daughter into our home. Our new daughter is very precious to us. She has been a joy to watch as she learns to do something new every day. She now rolls over both ways and is beginning to hold her bottle by herself. She likes to chew on her hands but she doesn't suck her thumb. We have been lucky none of our children have been thumb suckers.

Your/our daughter has been very healthy. She weighs 17 pounds at the present time. She is a beautiful child with a fantastic disposition. She sleeps all night without waking usually. Occasionally she wakes up at night but all she does is giggle herself back to sleep.

Thank you for allowing me to be her adoptive father. I promise you that I will give her all the love I have to give. She will be raised as a Christian in a Christian home. I will do everything I can to prepare her for a complex world. She will be made aware of who she is, and we will do all we can to help her become a whole and complete person. We love her more than you can imagine.

We pray for you constantly. Please don't worry about her. She is happy, well, and loved very dearly.

God Bless You
Your child's Adoptive Father

TWO SETS OF PARENTS

> Adoption is the process of accepting the responsibility of raising an **individual who has two sets of parents.**

The final aspect of our definition of adoption emphasizes that adoptive parents do not own the adoptee. Whether we give birth to our children or adopt them, children are individuals and not our possessions to forever hold close. We emphasize this primarily as a reminder because adoptive parents tend to protect and cling to the child they struggled so long to find.

All parents experience some anxiety as their child matures and approaches the age when he will leave home. Physical separation, however, is only one aspect of the anxiety adoptive parents feel. At some point, adoptive parents may have to cope with the additional fear of an emotional separation from their child—more specifically, they fear that their child will eventually reject them in favor of those "other parents." We often hear this fear phrased, "If my child searches for her birthparents, I will have been nothing more than a babysitter all these years" (fourth myth revisited). A more subtle expression of the same fear is, "If I have a good relationship with my daughter, she will still love me if she finds her birthmother."

Both statements reflect a belief that adoptive parents always risk losing their child. No matter how much they may wish away this fear, adoptive parents can not change the existence of another set of parents for their child. Love for a child is a commitment to raise the child, not to cut that child off from the people who partly represent his past and his future.

We can not say if the adoptee will have disturbing questions about the individuals who gave him life, his physical appearance, and inherited potential. We do not know if the adoptee will need to search for his heritage and touch a piece of that reality. We are convinced, however, that we can prepare our adoptive parents for these possibilities. This preparation includes examining the origin of the adoptive parents' apprehensions. For some adoptive parents, their fears stem from the second-best feelings left in the aftermath of their infertility or sudden confrontation with the realities of adoption. Certainly a parent has a more difficult time sustaining an "as if she were my daughter" pretense when that daughter is actively searching for "other parents."

Once we examine the emotions involved, we find that parents can provide their children honest answers and assistance without a sense of failure. By facing their own fright of emotional separation, our parents can better accept their child's need to have a whole identity. Of course that means knowing the people who gave her life. The following excerpt from a letter written by an adoptive mother to her daughter's birthmother illustrates our point:

> . . . Shannon you don't have to worry about Leslie knowing you love her. We know what a sacrifice you've made and we intend to tell her how much you loved and cared for her. I'll see that she gets your letter, pictures, and the lovely blanket. We won't have to compete for her love. I'm sure she'll hold a special spot for each of us. We love you for the life you've given us and we'll see that Leslie shares our feelings.

I don't have a picture to send now. I want to send one of her smiling. I will try to send you one soon.

We hope your adjustment will go as easy as Leslie's has. I think of you often as I hold my very special and very wonderful daughter.

Julie

It is quite normal for children to want to know about their heritage. No matter how much love adoptive parents give their children, a certain curiosity remains. That curiosity has nothing to do with the child's love for the adoptive parents. We are convinced that when adoptees do find their birthparents, the result usually relieves everyone. After the mystery is solved, the adoptee is freed to move on with his own life, and his adoptive parents finally learn they will not be rejected. Feelings of frustration and doubt are erased.

Consider, for example, how the adoptee and parents might feel after meeting Stephanie, the sensitive birthmother who wrote the following two letters:

My Dearest Tara,

I'm writing this letter to you so I can tell you about me and also explain my reasons for not keeping you. First, a little bit of my history. I gave birth to you at the age of 19. You are the best thing that ever happened to me. I have lots of hobbies. They are swimming, horseback riding, reading mysteries, and snow/water skiing. Enough of that. I need to tell you my reasons now. Please don't think that I don't love you because I didn't keep you. I didn't keep you, well its hard to explain. But I will try anyway. I need to set it straight. I was young to have a child but I still wanted to go through with it. Also, your father and I weren't ready for marriage and a baby at the same time. They are very big responsibilities. I wanted very much to keep you and to raise you myself but you needed both a mom and a dad who already have a home and will see that you get a good education, and lots and lots of love between the parents and for you and your brother.

I do love you very, very much. I have so much love for you that you just can't describe it in words. You are always in my prayers and thoughts every-day. I know they're taking real good care of you and also God is watching out for you too. Fortunately, I was able to get to see you till you were 3 weeks old. Your were such a good baby. You weighed 11 lbs and 4 oz. and were 22 1/2 in. long. Also you came 2 weeks late. But I didn't mind, it was well worth it. You are such a joy to me. I'm just sorry I wasn't able to raise you When I get married I know I'll have more children but you were my first and are the most precious of all. I will never forget you. When you're old enough and you would like to find me, that would make me very happy, if that is what you want to do. Giving you up was the most hard-est decision that I ever had to make. But Tara, I was only thinking of your future and welfare. May hap-piness always come your way. I wish you all the luck in the world. Always remember I love you very much. I know you'll be very happy with your fam-ily. They love you very much too. Look up to your big brother. I'm sure he'll give you good advice as you get older.

> I Love You,
> Your mom, Stephanie

Dear Parents,

I am now getting around to writing ya'lls let-ter. It's not that I have been putting it off or any-thing, its just that this is not an easy thing for me to do. In fact, writing this letter to ya'll is very important to me. It really means an awful lot to me. When I was 3 months pregnant and I knew Tara's father wouldn't be getting married, I then realized adoption was the best positive step that I could have made for my baby and myself. I didn't know a lot about adoption but I sure know a lot more now than I did at first. I know in my heart that I made the right decision and I'm awfully glad that you and your husband are happy with your new addition to the family.

Ya'lls autobiographies were nice and thats why I selected you to be the parents of my baby. I'm sure you know that I wanted to keep her but she does need a mom and dad. Besides, on my salary right now I wouldn't be able to give a whole lot to her except lots of love and care. I think that is most important. My social worker has told me what a good baby she is. She was that way in the hospital too. I'm very proud of her. She is my pride and joy, even though I won't get to see her grow up into a grown woman. She'll always be very precious to me. I love her very much and I would like for ya'll to know that. When you do start to tell Tara she is adopted and if she asks questions about me please remember I love her and that I was thinking of her future. I do not want her growing up thinking I don't love her. . . .

During labor with Tara wasn't too hard. Every now and then the pain was just a little unbearable. But after 17-1/2 hours she finally came. That was the proudest moment in my life. God really helped me select a good set of parents. Thank you for wanting her and for loving her enough to adopt another child. Ya'll are very special people to me. Pat and Betty [two adoptive mothers] were with me during labor and that made it a lot easier for me when it got really rough. Betty even got to see her head crown. That's something Betty has never been able to experience and so it was special to her and to me. I spent a month at the maternity home but I did not enjoy it all that much but I'm thankful that there is a place that we could go to when we didn't have any other.

Do you think it would be alright to get another picture of Tara please? I enjoy looking at her pictures and looking back on the times I was able to spend with her. It does not depress me. So please don't think that. To tell you the truth, it helps me get through the day when I think of her or even talk about her with my friends. I am giving you 2 pictures that were taken down at the agency office. I would like for Tara to have them please. Well I guess I've written all I can for right now. Another thing, ongoing correspondence will be just fine with me. My thought and prayers are with you. May God be with you always.

Stephanie

In total, our definition of adoption implicitly declares the adoptee as our primary client, while emphasizing the equal role of his two sets of parents. Each parent has contributed to the person the adoptee is or will become. The interaction among these three parties has been referred to as an adoption triangle. Although a triangle best indicates the three-sided relationship, we would add to this concept. We would place the adoptee at the apex of the triangle to signify the fact he brought the triangle together, and correctly focus our attention on his needs. His parents we would place on an equal level below, one set not displacing the other. The result is a picture of five people fate has tied together.

As previously detailed, each individual in our triangle experiences separate losses and unique pains. Adoptive parents experience the grief caused by their infertility and consequential sadness because they can not be "total" parents. Birthparents sustain the dramatic loss of the parental role of nurturing and shaping their child. Finally, the adoptee loses because he will never know what it is like to totally belong to only one mother and one father. To deny the invisible ties of emotion that bond them together would be to live a lie.

Three final letters in this chapter are offered to illustrate just how strong these ties of emotion can be for the individuals daily involved in the adoption drama. The first letter was written by an adoptive mother who has accepted the fact that adoptive parents have no guarantees the child will accept them forever, with never a thought of the people who gave him life. This mother sought a child through the process of adoption to love and nurture. She has assumed all the responsibility that role places on her, and she has done so while fully acknowledging "another mother."

Dear Penny,

I have been thinking of you so much, especially since we have celebrated Brandi's 1st birthday. I just know you were thinking of her too.

She started crawling at 9 months and getting into everything. Now she is walking around furniture or if you hold her hands. Her eyes light up with the feeling of accomplishment as she walks. She's very responsive—expressive—you can imagine what she's thinking and chabbering about. Stands on her tip toes alot, like a little toe dancer. Sometimes balances on one leg while lifting the other. Guess she's going to start climbing soon. Tried to follow her brother up on his bed—fell and looked like she might have her first black eye. It's O.K., just a little redness—don't worry she is a very normal, inquisitive child. She thinks it's real funny to climb up on her brother and pull his hair. She loves to laugh and sometimes fakes laughter for attention. Can cry and squeal real loud too. . . .

I am enclosing a copy of a book that really touched my heart and I pray that it will help you if you ever experience feelings as shared in the book.

I hope you know that you always have the right to be in touch with us or the agency concerning Brandi. And it helps us to know if Brandi ever had a medical emergency, we could find out about heritage via the agency. We pray too that you will stay in touch with the agency so that when Brandi reaches maturity age and if she wants to contact you and if agreeable with you, she would be able to. I pray that you and Brandi never have to suffer some of the pain and anguish shared in S. Musser's book.

I have enclosed some pictures of Brandi. As you can see, she is a joy.

What are your plans for the future? Did you complete high school or are you starting your senior year? Hope you are well.

Remember—there is a family you haven't met who cares for you.

God bless you,
Roger and Di
Bill and Brandi

Birthparents will have no memories of the excitement of their child's first step, the anxiety of his first day of school, or the wistful sadness of his graduation from high school. They relinquish that nurturing parental role. They do not, however, abandon all responsibility. Birthparents, like the following birthmother, neither forget their children nor do they want to abdicate whatever role they have in assuring continued security and happiness for their children.

To Clark's Parents,

I'm very glad you were able to write and send me pictures of Clark. I'm very happy to know that he is being taken very good care of. From those ear to ear smiles I can see he is very happy and happiness is what I always wanted for him.

I'm glad to know he enjoys his big brother so much. I hope they become very close to each other as they grow. That would enrich their lives so.

I see the resemblance now between us. He has my face and his birthfather's muscular body. Clark sounds like he's going to be an energetic little boy once he starts walking.

It was a happy surprise that you named him Clark. That was the second name I had in mind for him. It is one of my favorite names.

It's a good feeling to know that all is going well
and that Clark is growing up the way all little boys
should. I hope you keep in touch because it makes
me happy to know what a happy and healthy boy
he's growing up to be. Please give him a kiss for me
and tell him I miss and love him very much. Thank
you so much for the letter and the pictures. I really
do appreciate it. I'm always hoping only for the best
for you and your little family.

Clark's birth mother

When the adoptee finally knows both sets of parents,
why should anyone be threatened? If the adoptee grows to
love them both, that will not diminish either relationship. Love
for one individual is not lessened because we also love
another. If knowing and loving gives the adoptee peace of
mind, everyone should welcome that opportunity. The child's
happiness is the parents' happiness, because the child is the
apex of the adoption triangle.

Dear Birthmother,

This has been, at the same time, the most difficult and the easiest letter that we have ever had to
write. It is easy to express our love for the baby and
our appreciation to you for allowing us to share in
that love. It is only the wording which makes it difficult. We keep wondering if phrases like "your
baby" or "our baby" will cause anxiety, whereas
"the baby" seems so very impersonal. We hope that
you will realize that when we refer to "our baby"
that you will always be considered as part of that
"our," for you will always be a part of her as well as
our lives.

It is hard to express how thrilled we were
when we received the phone call telling us that our
long wait for a baby was finally over. It was, however, nothing compared with the thrill of seeing her
for the first time. She is the most beautiful baby girl
that we have ever seen. It is possible, I supposed,
that we are slightly prejudiced towards her, but

that cannot be all of it, as everyone we meet has the same reaction to her. She is not only beautiful, but she is also the sweetest baby that has ever been. She already has such a happy personality, and she is so alert to everything around her. She is amazed by everything she sees and seems completely at ease with every situation.

We know that you must have put a lot of love into the nine months that she was with you, for she could not be any more perfect than she is. She is also very healthy—with not so much as even a simple skin rash. You have enriched our lives far more than any of us can possibly express. Her new brother, who is six, is as excited about her as we are so there will be no end to the amount of love that she will receive.

We hope that you will not feel any sadness upon receiving this letter. You are responsible for so much joy that we hope that some of that joy will be a part of your life as well.

We have enclosed a picture of "our" little girl and her brother. We also wanted to let you know that we had a lovely Baptism service for her on November 9th. We want to wish you the very best that life can bring for you, and express our deepest appreciation for the great joy that you have brought into our lives.

Your friends always,
The Adoptive Parents

9
Openness –
The Opportunity
To Share Love

Dear Birthmother and Friend,

    This is a picture of "our" dear little one. We couldn't let Christmas pass without sharing with you our thoughts and our love. . . .

> Excerpt from a letter
> written by two adoptive
> parents

Since that first letter exchange demanded by a single birth-mother, we have taken some big steps forward. Our first step was learning how four myths clouded our thinking and stagnated our adoptive practices. We subsequently abandoned all myths and reevaluated traditional approaches. In the process, our clients taught us to design a program that responds to the needs of all five individuals in the adoption drama. Today, our practices are based on one simple theory:

Individuals handle their lives and their destinies best when addressed with trust and honesty instead of protective secrecy and half truths.

Therefore, we prepare our clients to face the lifetime experience of adoption with faith in themselves and trust for the other members of their triangle.

When we first wrote this book (1980-1982) we avoided the phrase "open adoption" because we were told the term would panic our readers. Since then our clients have convinced us that words do not frighten people; rather, new ideas colliding with preconceived myths frighten people. Individuals who practice traditional adoption or who have experienced a closed adoption often respond to our ideas with skepticism, resentment, or even anger. These reactions are understandable because open adoption directly clashes with the secrecy mandated by the second myth. Although we fully understand and appreciate the cognitive dissonance our approach initially evokes, we no longer hesitate to proudly state that we practice open adoption.

In part, our position is explained by our basic belief that people deal with the truth more quickly and more effectively than with dressed-up words chosen to soften responses, words which also may be chosen to blur realities. We hope this book will serve to enlighten adoption perspectives and assure the reader of the favorable outcomes of open alternatives.

The next question, of course, is how open is "open?" We quickly progressed beyond the simple letter exchanges which we have shared with you in this book to face-to-face meetings, sharing full identifying information (full names and addresses), and ongoing contact over the years. The type and frequency of ongoing contact is determined by the individuals involved in each adoption, but contact ranges from letters and pictures to visitation. In this, our final chapter, we will share these added dimensions of openness.

SHARING NAMES

Today, open adoption includes sharing full names. However, when we began sharing names, we limited this sharing to first names only (unfortunately many agencies call this practice open adoption, while it is, in fact, semi-open adoption). Although it is now difficult for us to remember the depth of our professional concern, we initially worried about and thoroughly discussed the impact of name exchanges. We assumed birthparents and adoptive parents would both be reticent about exchanging such identifying information. We soon learned that the participants thought differently. Both birthparents and adoptive parents eagerly sought names to erase forever impersonal labels—"your birthparents," "the adoptive parents," "the baby." Somehow, knowing the real names of all the players in their particular adoption story facilitates interaction and intimate sharing among our families. No catastrophes, not even minor injuries, have occurred in the aftermath of what once looked like a great risk. This should serve as a lesson to agencies and other intermediaries who continue to practice semi-open adoption, rather than evolving to fully open adoptions.

Our evolution in exchanging names is an excellent example of how the process and tension of deciding whether to accept an open practice is dramatically overstated when contrasted to its matter-of-fact acceptance today. Now all parties consider name exchanges as a minimum. In fact, letters that are not addressed to a named person now seem unnatural. The following two letters (and other letters in this chapter), which demonstrate our early name exchanges, chronicle our evolution to increased openness:

> Dear Bobbie,
>
> It is very difficult for us to write this letter because we have so many thoughts and so few words to express those thoughts. You gave us the most precious thing in our lives. For this, a simple "thank you" seems so little.
>
> Instead of trying to find some way to tell you how grateful we are for the opportunity to adopt your birthchild, let us instead tell you that he is an extremely happy and contented child. We believe that this happiness begins to develop long before a child is ever born. From you he got this, and that will shape so much of his life. He accepts and gives love so readily with a big smile and sparkling blue eyes.
>
> We appreciate the little stuffed bear and the bear bank that you sent. It is really more than coincidence that you should send bears. You see, we named our son Barret. His room is filled with bears of all sizes and descriptions because his

grandfather has already nicknamed him "Bear." In addition to a life-line you have also given him a love-line, and he will be very much aware of this as he grows up.

You are in our prayers, Bobbie, and we hope for you the same happiness that you have given us.

God bless you,
Jenny and John

Dear Jenny and John,

I understand how you feel when you say you cannot express your thoughts and feelings with words. There can be no comparison. You are constantly in my thoughts. I feel very lucky to have such a loving couple as you raise the child I gave birth to. I was so glad to hear he is so happy and loving, and also that he is doing well. I feel his being happy has to do with the environment surrounding him and you have given him that. I would like to thank you for your letter and the picture, I shall treasure them always.

I hope that you won't harbor thoughts of me turning up on your doorstep to take Barret home with me. I have talked to many adopting parents who had this fear. Barret is now your child and no matter what I may feel in the future I will not come searching for him, that choice will be his when he gets older. If he ever decides he feels the need to come and find me, my door will always be open wide for him and you. I feel that as his real parents you are part of me. . . .

I love Barret very much and I know in my heart no one can raise him as well as you can. . . . I have no regrets where Barret is concerned. Of course, I feel, as I'm sure many birthmothers do, that I could have kept him. The Lord had other plans for Barret and myself and we were not meant to be together. I want you to know that when I find that special someone to share my life with, he will know as much as I do about Barret because I want a totally honest relationship. I am not now nor ever will be ashamed of the part I played in giving Barret life. He is a part of me and always will be.

I feel that it's more than coincidence that you named him Barret. I couldn't have given him a better name myself. It seems odd for me to send him bears before I knew his name and what it meant. When I did find out I was pleasantly surprised. I will always think of him as my little (well maybe not so little) "Bear." There is so much more I would like to say but a letter is not the place for it. Words just seem so inadequate for all my feelings and thoughts. I'll just say I love you both and I wish you total happiness in your future. Perhaps with Barret you can find that happiness.

God Bless You,
Bobbie

ONGOING SHARING OF LETTERS AND PHOTOGRAPHS

Our initial letter exchanges contemplated only one exchange in the period immediately following placements. Although we were proud of our "progressive" practice, we never considered that either set of parents might desire continued contact. Adoption triangle members have since taught us differently. Today, the number of periodic letter exchanges depends on the individuals involved in each case. Most of our clients now communicate on a regular basis, the child's birthday and Christmas being special days. Letters exchanged usually focus on developmental information about the adoptee and expressions of concern and assurance between the two sets of parents. The following letter is a good example of both. The letter was written by a young adoptive couple to their son's birthmother one and one-half years after Alan's placement. They sought to update Irene about Alan, since their first letter had been written when Alan was only four months old:

Dear Irene,

Please forgive this late overdue letter. We think of you daily and pray for your happiness. But we live out of state now by our families and Alan is so attached to his grandparents and cousins. He is the only grandson on his dad's side of the family. He can do no wrong with them.

Alan is such a happy little boy. He loves to flirt with girls in the stores. They comment on his dimple and he winks at them. His favorite toys are tonka trucks and books on trucks.

His health had been excellent this year. Last year he had a few ear infections. He is a very active little guy. We joke about him either taking something apart; trying to plug it in; or putting it back together. He's very coordinated for his size. We think he will be a good athlete if that's what he wants. He has a very good memory for things he has seen and then tries it at a later time. He really keeps us on the go, and we love it.

Alan has made our family so complete. His sisters love him, and he goes to them for protection if he is in the wrong. Alan is a wonderful little boy that you can be very proud of. He also has a very kind side that loves little babies and shares very well.

He goes once a week to a play group. If another child cries, Alan will pat that child's back or kiss them. His teacher is very impressed by his thoughtfulness at this early age.

A simple "thank you" just isn't enough for this wonderful little boy. You can be sure we'll try to raise him to be a happy well adjusted child and to have a healthy understanding of his adoption. We feel very strong that Alan will love you just as we do as he matures. May God be with you and your family. Have a happy holiday.

Happy Holidays,
Betty and Stan

Birthparents who receive updates about their child cherish the information and the warmth of the letters. For some who feel isolated from society for being unwed parents, these letters become their only outlet for their continued caring. Dawn responded to a letter from her child's adoptive parents by assuring them she did not intend to infringe on their family's happiness, but was thankful to them for "showing me that the biggest decision of my life that I had to make was the right one . . ."

Dearest Nancy and Terry,

I can't begin to tell you how much fulfillment and happiness your letter and darling pictures brought to me.

Your letter relieved a lot of thoughts and most important my decision to relinquish "our son." I agree very strongly that Drew is our baby. I brought Drew into this world and you gave him a home of love, happiness and health. I couldn't ask for anything more.

Drew is a beautiful baby. I thank you so very much for the pictures. I can see by the smile on his face he is indeed a happy, content and healthy little boy. I will treasure Drew's pictures and your very kind and thoughtful letter for a very long time.

Your letter was just that very kind and thoughtful. I especially appreciate you sharing with me, how Drew is progressing with his first two years of life.

There also is rarely a day that goes by, I don't think of Drew, now I can add his parents to my thoughts with thanks of knowing that Drew will receive nothing but the best throughout his life.

I want you to understand that you will receive no trouble from me and I would deeply appreciate it if you would stay in touch every so often, and would share a few of Drew's pictures with me. I know that is a lot to ask and I'll understand if you don't agree. It's just a wonderful feeling seeing what an adorable child Drew is and know that the three of you are doing fine. For the three of you are a big and important part of my life. My hopes and prayers will always be with you.

At one time I was considering writing Drew a letter to be put away until his 18th birthday, explaining the reason why I gave him up for adoption. I have now changed my mind. I have only one favor to ask of you, and that is to explain to Drew, for me, when the time is right, or best, the reason I made the decision, and that was, because at seventeen I couldn't of provided him with a proper home, nor a father figure, he left long ago. The love for Drew was so strong at that time, that Drew came first. That's when I made my decision to let go of Drew and give him to a couple who could give him all the love and comforts of a home and the joys of life. I will never expect Drew to think of me as a mother, for you are the only parents he'll grow to know and love. I do want Drew to understand I did and do love him, and because of that I wanted to give him the best which I am convinced I did.

My life has gone on. I just finished a year of college and plan on transferring over to a business college. I also plan to marry in a years' time and am looking forward to starting a family of my own in the future.

My mother wants to send her thanks for the pictures and the letter. She thought Drew's pictures were darling, and the letter was very considerate. Yes, I have faith in God, for he gave us Drew. I, too, agree we'll all be Drew's parents in heaven.

May God Bless and Watch over you and Drew.

Thank you, Thank you for showing me that the biggest decision of my life that I had to make was the right one and it gave happiness to three other people, Drew, Nancy and Terry. God Bless and Be with you. All my love and gratitude.

Dawn

P.S. Drew is a beautiful name. I really like it.

In turn, adoptive parents like Nancy and Terry enthusiastically seek ongoing correspondence with their son's birthmother. The reasons include a desire to repay the birthmother for her gift of a child and the hope that such open communication will benefit their child's growth and identity.

Ongoing correspondence also provides the adoptee access to a complete genealogical history, and current medical records of both the birthmother and the birthfather. The following letter is one in the series of exchanges Nancy and Terry have shared with Dawn. Their letter (in answer to another one of Dawn's letters) is typical of the concern and love we see shared:

Dear Dawn,

We were so excited, so curious, so delighted and so touched to get your letter!! You are so pretty and Drew looks so much like you!

We are going to keep one picture out for Drew to see often and take one picture to a safe deposit box, along with your letters, for safe keeping.

It was so wonderful to hear all about your life now. It sounds as though things are really shaping up for you. Terry and I are really happy about your upcoming graduation and marriage. I know the new year is going to be your year!

Everything is very exciting here. Drew, Terry and I are anxiously awaiting a new baby that we are all adopting. Of course we don't know when the baby will come but we hope it's in time for Christmas! We tell Drew about adopting another baby but we're not sure he understands. But when we babysit our two month old niece, Kelly, Drew really enjoys her and is not jealous at all. Of course Drew has always been King around here! He was the first grandchild on my side and when relatives visit, "BOY," does he get the attention!

Drew is short for Robert Andrew which is his whole name. Everyone warned us that two years of age would be terrible. But on the contrary, this is Drew's cutest age ever! He can talk to us in a combination of words and gestures. He is <u>extremely</u> loving and kisses and hugs us constantly. Daddy is his favorite person and he imitates him perfectly. When Terry goes on trips (he's an airplane pilot) Drew says "Daddy flying" and makes a gesture and a sound like an airplane. He does this about ten times a day! He loves flying in airplanes and of course we travel a lot. Drew has been in many states. He's crazy about giraffes and goes wild over them at the zoo!

Terry and I are wondering whether we could love another child as much as we love Drew but both of our mothers assure us that we can (Terry's mom has 6 sons and my mom has 5 children).

We think of you daily, Dawn, and we pray for your well being. Especially when my sister-inlaw was pregnant and I saw her physical and emotional stages and I realized what you went through for Drew and for us. Never having been pregnant, I had never before realized the degree of sacrifice and love you must have experienced and felt. I guess we can never repay you fully. The one thing we can and will do is to raise "our" son to the very best of our abilities and give our all to this goal!

The more you write to us about you the more we grow in our love for you. Drew will be the most benefited from your letters, though. I can't wait until he's old enough to comprehend the love you have for him.

You have a very unique place in our lives. You gave Terry and me the gift of a life and for that we will always love you! Of course, we all know who ultimately gave us Drew, but you were His earthly counterpart.

It just proves that Romans 8:28 "God works all things together for good . . ." is true. I'm sure when you first found out you were pregnant, not much seemed good about it, but just look at the happiness you've brought us!

As for Drew's great pair of legs that you

referred to in your letter—What an understate-
ment—He has the cutest, strongest, chubbiest legs
ever.

Terry wanted to add to this but got called out
on a trip and we wanted to get this to you quickly!
But he'll write next time!

Have a wonderful Christmas! We love you.

Terry, Nancy and Drew

Our initial open practices carefully excluded identifying
information. Pictures of the baby were encouraged because
birthparents so obviously benefited. Babies change, however, so we somehow felt safe. What we did not realize at first
was how the myths still motivated us. We unconsciously
sought safe exchanges even though we no longer believed
secrecy was best. Actually, our adoptive parents sponta-
neously changed this by first sending current pictures of the
adoptee to birthparents, and then by venturing to request of
us current pictures of the birthparents. Today, our clients
share fully. Birthparents can choose to receive a variety of
pictures of their baby and pictures of his adoptive parents.
Adoptive parents, in return, can obtain pictures of their child's
birthparents and extended family members.

Once again, the afterglow of these picture exchanges
has been positive. Triangle members express delight in being
able to visualize each other as real people. Adoptive parents
remain the most enthusiastic, safeguarding the pictures for
their children. Many adoptive parents, in fact, place the birthparents' names and pictures in the adoptee's baby book.
These thus become an integral and natural part of that child's
story. Some adoptive parents put the birthmother's picture in
the baby's room—on his dresser or hanging on the wall (just
as other relatives pictures are displayed throughout the
house).

As we evolved with open adoption, so did most of our
previous clients. When Beverly and Kent adopted their
daughter Kelly, they were only interested in an initial letter.
Since then, as their letter demonstrates, they have done volunteer work with birthparents and read extensively on current
adoption controversies Their awareness of the benefits of

open approaches is reflected in the following letter to their birthparents, which is their third such letter:

> Dear Birthparents,
>
> I am sure this letter and these pictures out of the unexpected will surprise you. I sincerely hope they will be a happy surprise.
>
> In the past year we have become more involved in the adoption agency serving as a volunteer foster family for several young women as they waited for the birth of their babies. I'm sure this association has brought about a deeper understanding of birthmothers. I have also watched the changing procedures within the agency in regard to more openness between birthparents and adoptive families, openness which has included exchange of pictures, names and even face-to-face meetings.
>
> These experiences have resulted in wanting to share these pictures and in writing again to keep open communication. I am sure you must wonder about this beautiful daughter and how she is developing. I chose these pictures which were taken in April on an outing in the wildflowers at Canyon Lake because they are favorites of both her mother and father. One picture seems to capture the joyous spirit that she is and the other lets you see how beautiful she really is. I hope there is joy for you in these pictures. We would find joy in receiving pictures of you.
>
> We also have learned that you named your daughter Amy. This was shared by the foster family. I am thrilled to know this name and our daughter will know also that her "first" name is Amy. Did you give her a middle name? We have named her Kelly Anne.
>
> Our social worker also shared with us the news that you married. We were happy for you and wish you happiness and joy in your life together. We are appreciative of any information about you that we have in anticipation of all the questions

that Kelly will someday have and plan to be completely open with her in all that we know. I am also open to giving you continued updates on her development.

We are now in the process of applying for another baby so Kelly will not be an only child. We have been asked if we would be open to a face-to-face meeting with the birthmother. While the idea was initially unsettling, knowing how much I would love a face-to-face meeting with you I am hoping that opportunity will become a reality with the next child we adopt.

Our daughter is developing beautifully. She is into climbing these days. When I leave the room for a minute, it is not unusual to return and find her sitting in the middle of the table playing with whatever she found there "safely" out of her reach. She is saying lots of words such as wow, eye, bye bye, shoes, juice, grandma and so on. Unfortunately at this point her favorite seems to be "no" whether she means it or not.

Again, I want to express to you our gratitude for the chance to parent and love this most wonderful daughter of ours. So often we watch her and tell each other how rich we are. She is all we hoped for and more. We thank you and wish you joy and peace in your lives.

Sincerely yours,
Beverly and Kent

MEETING FACE-TO-FACE

When *Dear Birthmother* was initially published, only a few adoption agencies in the country allowed face-to-face meetings between adoptive parents and the birthparents of their baby at or near the time of placement. Today, most adoptions include at least a one-time face-to-face meeting, and progressive adoption programs offer open adoption (which includes meeting, sharing full identifying information, and having access to ongoing contact over the years). After many years of facilitating face-to-face meetings, we feel strongly that these meetings and direct ongoing contact benefit all adoption triangle members.

At the initial meeting, which is typically while the birthmother is still pregnant, all participants come together with respect for each other's role, and with some trepidation. Birthparents leave the meeting having learned more about the people who will provide the nurturing aspects of parenthood to their baby. As a result, birthparents do not have to labor under a lifetime guilt for having "abandoned" their child. They instead remember having actually participated in making responsible plans for that child's future.

One birthmother wrote the following love-inspired poem to the adoptive parents of her son after their face-to face meeting.

> I know we've only just met
> But feelings of love do exist,
> For circumstances of
>   future and past
> Have given opportunities
>   that our lives may share—
> And though our paths may vary,
>   We have a common goal
> For a child to grow happy
>   and healthy and wise—
> In a home that I have chosen.
>
>   D. L. Click
>   Birthmother

Adoptive parents also leave the meetings having learned more about the birthparents. Fears of mysterious strangers are dissipated, and remaining stereotypes of "those kinds of people" are effectively destroyed. Adoptive parents also learn valuable firsthand facts about the birthparent's interests and true personality, the kind of characteristics that can not be captured in a written social history. We often feel and hear their excitement in the simple statement, "I can tell my daughter I really met her birthmother."

The following note was written by an adoptive father

explaining his feelings about his initial meeting with Kim, his son's birthmother, shortly after the adoption:

> I was pleasantly surprised to find the birthmother of my adopted son, Daniel, to be prettier and more intelligent than I thought she would be. I don't know why I would have pre-conceived notions that she wouldn't be, unless I was preparing myself, in case she turned out to be that way.
>
> From my standpoint, it was a beautiful event of sharing information, getting to know and understand each other a little, and an opportunity I will never forget.
>
> I now have the opportunity of telling Daniel what his mother is really like. Of course she will grow and mature, but it may help him understand a little better why she had to give him up and that she could not have provided the kind of life for him that she really wants him to have, at least not at this time of her life.
>
> There didn't seem to be any barriers between us and it did help to find a subject that we all had in common besides the baby. That was cats! Once we hit that subject, we got into all sorts of topics, mostly about Kim.
>
> The experience of getting to know Kim will benefit our family for years to come and probably in some ways we haven't thought of yet. It seems to make the adoption process more complete and satisfying and I feel that Kim benefited greatly from the meeting too.
>
> The only thing that I found was different from what I expected was the fact that we didn't sit around and stare at each other for awhile before we could think of anything to say. It was easy to bring up subjects, ask questions, and give answers freely. . . .
>
> I want to thank the agency for giving us the opportunity to have this meeting. If they were not progressive in their ideas, we would not have had

this opportunity and we would never have gotten to
know a beautiful young woman named Kim.
Greg

Other adoptive parents who have met with their birthparents have spoken in the same positive terms as Daniel's
adoptive father. To date they have expressed only one disad-
vantage. Without exception they have all encountered from
family members and friends troubled reactions to these meetings. They have often heard such comments as "Aren't you
afraid that, now that she knows who you are, she will come
get your baby back?" or "I could never do that!" By contrast,
the parents who have had the most direct experience, felt
reassured and comfortable with their meetings. They have
had the unique opportunity to see and hear their birthparents
personally say, "I won't interfere," or "I no longer feel that she
is just my baby," or "I love you both."

One adoptive father emotionally touched by the experience of meeting his son's birthmother wrote a letter to his son
to be read and appreciated at some future date. He and his
wife first met the birthmother, Lori, during her pregnancy, visited with her and the baby in the hospital, and continued to
visit after the adoption (Lori came to spend her Easter
vacation with them). They plan to continue with regular visits
and correspondence over the years. The letter captures the
adoptive father's affection and trust for the woman who is
Neil's birthmother:

Dearest Neil,
    As your mother and I look at your smiling,
happy face, our thoughts rush out to another
happy, smiling face in our lives. Your birthmother,
Lori, is a wonderful, beautiful person who has
become an important part of all of our lives.
    We will always remember the day we first met
Lori. She was far more nervous than your mother
or I. She after all, had read our autobiographies,
and was certain that she would like us. She was
afraid, however, that we would reject her and not
feel comfortable raising her child.

We did not know very much about her beyond the brief background information given to us by our social worker. We did see a picture of your birthparents, and were impressed with how handsome they looked together.

Lori did not stay nervous very long. She is such a warm, outgoing person that she rapidly put everyone at ease. It was so easy to like Lori, after all, she has your dimples and smile.

Lori was very concerned about your future and for that reason she selected your mother and I to raise you. Lori wanted you to be loved and to be raised by parents who shared her interests in athletics and education. She wanted you nurtured by a family that would love you as much as she does.

We want you to appreciate how exciting it was for your mother and I to again visit you and Lori the day after your birth. That time in the hospital is special and is shared by very few adoptive families. Lori was so proud of you when she took us to the nursery to see you. We remember how small you were and what a tight bundle the nurses had made of you and your blankets. Your mother was worried that we would not find you as beautiful as Lori did. We worried that Lori's pride in you was caused by her love for you, but as soon as we saw you we knew that Lori had every right to be proud. You were a very beautiful, healthy baby. Lori told us how much you looked like pictures she had seen of her sister and herself as babies.

The next day was very special for our new family. Lori brought you from the hospital to the agency where your mother and I waited. We had a ceremony during which Lori presented you to us and asked us to love you and care for you.

You know that your mother and I correspond with Lori very often. She has become part of all our lives and will always play a role in your life. The pictures and letters we exchange with one another are treasured by all of us. She has become a good friend who shares our love for you.

Your mother and I are very comfortable with our lives as adoptive parents. We are proud of you and relate the story of your adoption to anyone who asks. Some people, who hear our story for the first time, are troubled because in the past birthparents and adoptive families were not allowed to correspond or meet face to face. When they understand our story, and learn how important it is for you to know about the couple who gave you birth, they realize that adoption affects more than just three people. It affects the adoptive parent's family and the birthparent's families. Communicating with your birthparents keeps their families aware of your development. Hopefully this will draw all of our families closer together. Our closeness will make it easier for you to receive answers to the questions you will have as you grow older.

We want you to always know that many people love you. Among those who love you most are your mother and I and a very special young woman who loved you very much when you were born and who loves you still. We know when you are older you will return the love that all of us have invested in you.

All our love,
Your parents

Kathy Giles, who adopted two boys, shares her initial fears and evolution to meeting the birthmother of her first son:

Our first adoption started as a "closed" adoption. I like to describe our entrance into open adoption as "We didn't know there was such a thing as open adoption, and then we were one!" I recall my frustration that a good friend of mine personally knew the 14-year-old girl who was carrying what would be our baby. She even let her name slip. . . Judi. Her name is Judi. Out there somewhere was this young girl named Judi, and she was carrying my baby. Why could my friend know her, and I couldn't? Didn't Judi and I have more reason to know each other? But convention forbade our knowing each other. For five months I prayed for my baby, but the birthmother seemed more real to me . . . and my prayers often turned to be centered on her. In the last month I couldn't sleep. When I would awake, my thoughts would turn to her. "Somewhere out there Judi is probably having trouble sleeping, too. If she can't sleep, why should I?"

When the baby was born, the lawyer called and told us we had a son. I was dumb-founded. A boy!!!? How could it be? I thought for sure the baby was a girl! Oh, well. So we took him home from the hospital, filed papers to adopt, and fell in love with our little prince.

Two months later through a series of miraculous events, we learned that Judi had a legal right to know who she was giving her baby to, and she wanted to exercise that right. We would meet. All my desire to know her turned to fear. "When they see him, how beautiful he is, they will want him back." Then we met. Later I would say that I was so glad I didn't have Jonathan in my arms as Judi came down the hall toward me. My arms were fully ready to receive the "girl child" of my prayers. She was the first child of my heart. As I opened my arms, she freely came into them. Holding her, crying tears of joy over her, was the most natural thing in the world.

When we began to offer face-to-face meetings, many of our past adoptive parents and birthparents who did not get this opportunity expressed an interest in meeting one another. One such couple, Terry and Nancy, whom we met earlier in this chapter, invited their first birthmother to meet with them after they had the experience of meeting with the birthmother of their second child, Sarah. The letter that Dawn, the birthmother, wrote in response to Terry and Nancy's unexpected request dramatically speaks of the bond of love these individuals so freely and comfortably want to share:

Hi Terry, Nancy and Drew,

Let me congratulate you on the new addition, Sarah Beth, what a beautiful name for such a beautiful little girl. She is adorable. I'm so happy to hear that Drew adores her and there is no sign of jealousy. I know that makes it a lot easier on the whole family.

No, I couldn't believe that you got to meet Sarah's birthmother. Wow, that's great, I mean that is wonderful. I'm still a little shocked. How I wish that I would of had that privilege. I'm not really jealous of the fact that Gail met with you and saw Sarah, but I am serious, I actually cried when I read in your letter that I could meet you and see Drew. Oh, Terry and Nancy I need no time to think whether or not I would like to meet with you and Drew (and of course I would love to meet Sarah, after all she is Drew's sister).

That has been my biggest prayer and dream and one of my most thought of thoughts. I would love to meet with you. The only problem is it can't be right now. It would have to be either this summer say August or this winter around November. If that could be arranged. The reason is one school, I don't graduate till June. Then hopefully I will get a job. Job means money and money means my plane ticket to San Antonio. Would that be okay with you. You know that I will try to meet with you as soon as possible. I think this is wonderful. You don't know how happy it would make me feel. I feel that since we all feel that we know each (in my opinion) other quite well, we would have little, maybe even no trouble picking up the pieces. I'm sure we'd feel comfortable. In your letter (it was a lovely letter I read it 2 times then I read it to my mom!) you said meet now, please let me know if August or November—somewhere in between there would be too late to make our arrangements. It's the best I can do, I hope and pray that it will all work out. It's all we've been thinking about. If you'd like you can also tape our conversation. Ask anything you'd like, especially anything concerning Drew and his future because you are the only ones I would talk to about Drew's natural father. Listen to me I'm so excited, I better stop getting so carried away and wait to hear what you have to say about our arrangement. I just know there is nothing I want more than to meet Drew and talk to him, hold and kiss him and meet the two most very special people that God has given to me.

I also feel deep down in my heart that there is a bond between Gail and I. I feel that she is very special. We've both been through the same situation, experienced the same experiences, and were both blessed with beautiful healthy babies that God put into the care of two wonderful people named Nancy and Terry. I too feel that God put us together ultimately and I love Him that much more for His miracles.

I love the two pictures that you sent me. Drew has grown, I should say is growing. He looks like he's a little taller than most boys his age. He is so cute. My mother said she thought the picture of Terry, Drew and Sarah was adorable. She especially liked your caption on the back. Nancy, if I haven't mentioned it before my mother is also very comfortable with our situation. We often sit down and talk for hours about my pregnancy and how happy Drew looks in his pictures. Our favorite conversation is talking about how cute Drew is.

She has been a big help to me especially when I returned home from San Antonio. We would talk, she was mainly concerned with how I was going to deal with the act after relinquishing our son. She says she is very proud of me for my decision and how I've handled myself. She too was hurting at first after all Drew at that time may of been her grandson. Now she feels that God worked it all out for the best. I'm the kind of person who likes to talk things out. I don't hold things in. My being like this has opened many doors for me. Giving birth to Drew made me realize many things most of all I have learned and matured from that. I know that I am going to do my darndest to fulfill my life and those involved and around me. Life is too precious to waste. I have high hopes for me starting a family. May I (when the time comes to start a family) share this with you. You will always be with me for the rest of my life (you won't be able to get rid of me, I love you all too much).

Drew's nursery school seems like it is really neat—as you put it.

I was excited to hear that Drew's teacher said that he is well adjusted and secure. It's very important to me how Drew will adjust as he grows. I have total confidence in you. But it does make me feel great to hear comments about him, especially one as important as that was.

I know we said it over and over but I have to say it one more time. I am so glad God blessed Drew with a wonderful mother and father. I wouldn't want him with anyone else.

I hope this letter was understandable. My mind is still a little in shock about the new concept at the agency—Boy that's great. I do hope and pray we will meet, not right now, but real soon. (Hope!) I've got my fingers crossed.

Again, thank you for the picture of Drew and Sarah and Terry. They will be added to the rest. I will try to send pictures too.

> I love you lots,
> Dawn

SHARING FULL IDENTIFYING INFORMATION AND ONGOING VISITATION

Open adoption includes not only meeting one another, but also sharing full identifying information and ongoing contact over the years. The bond which develops between adoptive parents and birthparents continues beyond the time of the adoption, because these individuals care about one another (in fact, they even love one another). Therefore, they want to maintain a relationship with one another. In effect, as mentioned in *Children of Open Adoption*, they relate to one another like relatives. Yes, the birthmother is a relative because she is related to the child. Recognition of this fact is what open adoption is all about—accepting the birthparents (and their family) into your life as extended family members.

Adoptive parents Leslie and Steve Fitch have experienced this ongoing bond with their birthmother:

> We made contact with a woman whose second cousin was 8 months pregnant and looking for a couple. Kelly (birthmother) called us two days later. We immediately mailed her our Birthmother Letter and information about our agency. Kelly called us the day she received them and said she had chosen us as the parents for the child. We had a wonderful match meeting in the Los Angeles Office of our agency the next week, and Kelly gave us the ultra sound pictures of our future baby. Kelly, who was 20 at the time, knew she wasn't ready to parent, and she was lucky to have a loving family who supported her decision.
>
> Kelly decided to stay in California to give birth. After 18 hours of labor "shared" with both of us and Kelly's family, Leslie was the first to hold our beautiful Heather. Our love for her was instantaneous and only grows every day.
>
> We keep in contact with Kelly via photos, videos, and occasional phone calls. And Kelly came back to California to visit near Heather's first birthday. There was some awkwardness the first day, but openness, honesty, and respect on all of our parts made the rest of her week's stay very enjoyable, including Heather's first trip to Sea World.
>
> Kelly was always respectful to us; always

referring to Leslie as Mommy when she talked to Heather. While we know she is still experiencing some pain, Kelly seems very proud of her decision, and we are proud of her, too. When it's time for Heather to learn, she'll have proof that along with Mother and Father's love, there is a big dose of "Kelly Love," as well. What a great emotional investment in her future. We both know that love was already provided. . . the counseling allowed us to show it.

A few months after Larry and Darlene wrote their "Birthmother Letter" (Chapter 7), they were selected by a birthmother, Lisa, who was in the ninth month of her pregnancy at the time. They met and felt an instant bonding with one another. Darlene recalls some of their initial fears about open adoption and discusses the evolution of their special relationship:

> We signed up for an orientation meeting. . . . We walked out after four hours of listening intently, got in our car and said, "This isn't for us! No matter how bad we wanted a baby and to know the birthparents, this is crazy." The more we talked about it, we said let's give it a shot. We know so many people and family out of state that we would send our birthmother letter out of state, so we could match up with a birthmother from the east coast, fly her here to have the baby, and then fly her home. We thought this would be ideal for us. . . . We attended the two workshop sessions at the Center. We listened to the birthparents and adoptive parents (with open adoptions). My heart went out to them. You could feel all their emotions as though you had been through them yourself. . . .

The experience of the educational process and meeting their birthmother Lisa ("We all seemed so relaxed—as though we had known each other for years") changed their views dramatically. All of a sudden they were delighted to have a local birthmother (rather than one who would be 3000 miles away). They even invited Lisa to their first family baby shower shortly after Joey's birth, which also helped their families get to know and trust Lisa. Darlene recalls that as her family members were leaving the shower, "They all gave Lisa a hug and said 'Thank you.' But my greatest gift was watching my Mom and Larry's Mom both hug, kiss, and share tears with Lisa."

During the first few months post-birth, Darlene and Larry continued to visit with Lisa on a regular basis. In fact, they got upset when they didn't hear from Lisa as often as they wanted, so they bought her a telephone answering machine so they could leave messages telling her to call them!

Darlene and Larry have accepted Lisa into their lives as an extended family member, and they have a special love for her. Lisa worked through the normal feelings of grief much more easily because of her ongoing relationship with Joey and his parents. Joey reaps the benefit of having a relationship with both sets of parents.

Two years after Joey's birth, Lisa shared her feelings about their initial meeting and their ongoing relationship:

> I will never forget the first time I saw Larry and Darlene together. It was the day of our match meeting (initial meeting facilitated by the adoption counselor), and we had pulled in about the same time. I saw both of them, and I wanted to cry—not out of sadness, but because I wanted everything to be okay for them. I felt I loved them, and it was an instant bonding, and it was wonderful. Joey kept kicking inside me (inside my stomach) as if he was saying "Yes! Yes! Go for it!"
>
> I had prayed before to help me pick the right people. God really listened. I picked the best in my opinion. I thank God for them everyday. They gave me a new beginning, as I did for them. It was the most beautiful natural solution to my confusion, and my life was starting to fall together. I felt good about myself finally.
>
> The next morning Joey was born. I was

unsure if I even wanted to hold him. They brought this beautiful baby boy to my room. Larry held him first, I wanted it that way, since I truly believe in bonding. Besides Darlene was shaking like a leaf and hugging my mom. I was so happy for all of us.

They left about an hour later, and I decided to hold Joey. I held him, talked to him, and explained why. He looked as if he was saying, "I'm happy, it's okay, I understand."

If it had been a closed adoption, my heart would have been torn to pieces. I'd always be worried and wondering about him. With open adoption, I know he is so loved. My relationship with Larry and Darlene is incredible. I've gained a wonderful addition to my loved ones. We are like family. I call them about everything. They always support me and give me good advice, too. I can count on them. It's not as if I call them daily, drilling them on Joey's life. I call because I am loved and worried about. We get together about once a month.

We have a very loving, healthy relationship, and I feel very blessed. I love them all very much. If I hadn't become pregnant, I would have never met these 2 wonderful people who have enriched my life. I think trust is the key here.

P. S. Darlene and Larry you're the BEST!!

Eight years after Joey's birth, Darlene and Larry continue to have a close relationship with Lisa. They also adopted a second son, Matthew, two years after adopting Joey, and they have ongoing visitation with Matthew's birthparents, as well. Darlene relates her experience with both birthfamilies:

Our relationships with both of our son's birthparents have been wonderful. We all live in California, so it makes it really easy to speak and to see them once or twice a year. Both sets of birthparents have since married, and our boys have siblings. Now to our son Matthew (age 5), the word "half-sister" doesn't quite come across. He does understand the term "Birthmother." He has seen his half-sister twice and thinks she is cute, but that's about it for now. Actually, our son Joey (age 8) would really like to have a sister now, and thought it would be okay to ask his birthmother Lisa to do it for us—which we all (including Lisa) thought was so cute and innocent.

Darlene and Larry have also experienced a common phenomena, which is that the frequency of contact often declines over time after birthparents marry and are busy raising their own families. While many people who are considering open adoption assume they would be thrilled if the frequency of contact diminished over the years, in our experience most adoptive parents actually develop a close and caring relationship with their birthparents. They find that they *want* to maintain contact, both for themselves and for their child. As noted, Darlene and Larry visited with Lisa on a monthly basis for the first two years of their relationship; now they visit once or twice a year. Darlene shares her feelings about this change:

Having "limited" contact today has been hard for my husband and me. We are wishing for more contact. Our birthparents are not just "friends," but more like family members. We are trying to adjust to the fact that they are getting on with their lives, and our calls and visits are few and far between. Since our boys are older now, we feel more than ever the importance of our calls and visits with their birthparents.

Sandy, an adoptive mother, shared an early letter to their birthmother, Colleen, in Chapter 2. Now several years later, they continue to write to one another, talk on the phone ("It's been great to just pick up the phone and hear her voice or be able to call on special days"), and visit periodically. Sandy relates her feelings about their relationship and about Jed's (age 8-1/2) special birthday request:

In October Jed asked if we could go someplace special for his birthday month (November). When we asked him what he had in mind, he said he wanted to visit Colleen. . . .

Coleen suggested Sea World in San Antonio so neither of us would have to travel a long distance. It was a wonderful day for all of us with many talks, especially about what Colleen wanted for her future. . . .

She loved to compare Jed's special interests to those she had as a child and still has. There are many they have in common. . . .

We have a closeness that includes trust and concern for each other. We have all felt very comfortable with each other and have felt mutual respect.

Jed feels loved by Colleen and does not seem confused about her relationship to him. Our openness with Jed and Colleen has made our family relationship richer and has dispelled any fear or apprehension that we felt just before our first meeting.

Another adoptive mother, Caryl, shares their evolution from semi-open adoption to open adoption:

Seven and a half years ago, my husband and I would never have believed that we would ever invite our son's birthmother to our home for dinner along with her brother and his family, including her in our traditional celebration of the day we got him, nor think of her as part of our extended family. However, all of these things have occurred and more.

When we first agreed to an open adoption, we were willing to have one face-to-face meeting and to share letters anonymously through the adoption agency. Our first meeting occurred four days after the placement, and despite our anxiety and fear of the unknown, we immediately felt comfortable with John's birthmother. We found we had many similarities in our feelings regarding our own families, enjoyed the same activities, and placed the same value on many aspects of our lives. Corresponding with Colette, John's birthmother, served to deepen this relationship because we gradually began to realize that we were not adversaries but partners who wanted the same things for John: happy, loving relationships in which he would grow and find his own uniqueness.

This relationship developed as we grew to know and trust each other...We realized his under-standing of this (Colette's relationship to him) when he asked if we could invite her to our annual celebration of the day we got him. The importance of this risk for all of us is the way John has accepted the honesty and love that he has received. He enjoys knowing his birthmother and is a secure, happy child. As we look to the future, we have many questions and concerns about the effects on John and his acceptance of Colette; however, we do not have the fear we had seven and a half years ago. We feel confidence in our relationship and our abil-ity to adjust to John's changing needs.

Adoptive mother Kathy Giles, whom we met earlier in this chapter, speaks about her years of ongoing visitation with both of her sons' (Jonathan, almost 16, and David, age 10) birthparents:

Knowing the birthfamilies of my boys seems the most natural, normal thing in the world to me. I often take for granted all our family stuff and forget how special it is. Then I read a book about adult adoptees or birthmothers who never know how their child is, or I meet a grieving, bitter adult adoptee. Then I am suddenly shocked back into reality. I see clearly that what we have is special and wonderful and deserving of nurturing. Then I con-nect again with all the birthfamily and remind them that what we have is so special and that I value our relationships as treasures. And I remind myself and them that this is not just for us (although that would be enough for me). These relationships are for the boys, too. Ultimately, we are responsible to set in motion all that is needed for Jonathan and David to grow into healthy, whole adults.

As my oldest son, Jonathan, nears his 16th birthday, as I am ever so aware of his growing independence, I am keenly aware that adoption is not just about babies. It may start that way. There is all that hubba-hubba about a nursery, stroller, highchair, and car seat that are all color coordinated and matching. (I call this "the matching bumper pad and wallpaper/border phase.") The babies grow up. Adopted children do not stay children. They grow up. The real issues for the "big people" in their lives is will we assure they grow up healthy and whole? Or will we handicap and cripple them with secrets, barriers, possessiveness, and fear? I, for one, see myself in the former role. I'm the chief facilitator, the president of their fan club, and the head cheerleader (I write this in the first person because these are my feelings. In reality, these roles and objectives are completely shared and supported by my equally committed husband.)

BEYOND THE MYTHS

Because our evolution has been dramatic when contrasted to traditional adoptive practices, we have carefully evaluated each of our steps. Interestingly, whether it be letters, names, pictures, or meetings, the primary difficulty for the triangle members has been dealing with the comments of individuals outside the triangle—misguided friends, well-meaning family, and even some less progressive professionals. Our clients typically understand these comments and can patiently handle the reactions because they vividly remember when they too responded to adoption with the prejudices of the four adoption myths. Indeed, our triangle members become ambassadors and teachers to lead others to reject outmoded and often damaging ideas.

Epilogue

Our advocacy of open adoption practices often evokes two questions—whether from adoptive parents, physicians, judges, newspaper reporters, or casual on-lookers:

- Who really benefits from the openness?

- Won't open adoption have a chilling effect on the practice of adoption?

We answer the first question easily. The adoptee is our primary concern and stands to benefit most. As a child, he needs roots to grow, these being a permanent home and the security of a loving family. As an adult, he may need to know his genetic roots. Therefore, our task is to prepare both sets of parents. We want his birthparents to live with pride for the active participation they took in making responsible plans for their birthchild. We also want his adoptive parents to take pride in their status as parents. That includes having enough confidence in themselves and the adoptee's love to show him that they won't be crushed or think him ungrateful if he searches for the missing pieces of his own precious identity.

We address the second question by sharing the experiences and growth of the men and women living today's adoption stories. Our clients dramatically communicate to us that they are enriched and excited by our practices. It is possible for questioners or opponents to label our birthparents and adoptive parents as unique and special, saying, "These are not average individuals. They don't react the same way most people would in a similar situation." Not so. These are ordinary men and women, exceptional only in that they have had the opportunity to experience and react to adoption in a myth-free manner.

What we offer our readers—and society—is a workable approach to make future adoptions more humane and appropriately open in today's world. As we have witnessed open adoptions over the years since *Dear Birthmother* was initially published, we have become even more convinced that open adoption is healthier for all parties. We encourage our reader to seek out a professional intermediary who offers both open adoption and comprehensive counseling services. We feel that counseling, education, and support services are essential to a successful open adoption and should be an *integral* part of any adoption program.

We wrote this book partly to applaud adoptive relationships that are open and trusting. Adults seem to have more trouble with trusting. Children, on the other hand, appear naturally free in their acceptance and expressions. We feel the following three letters appropriately end our book. The first two letters were written by a nine-year-old and a seven-year-old to the birthmother of their new brother. In the simple and unabashed outpouring of real feelings, these two youngsters see adoption only as a wonderful opportunity to share love.

Dear BirthMother
thank you for letting us
adottopt   your baby
he is very   cute.
We LOVE him very
very very very very
very much. I like toomake
him laugh and make
him say words. He
is very healthy.
I like to see
him eat his
food cause
he is cute
then. trn it
over

I like to put him in to his baby swing and get him out of his bed and hold him to. I like to stroll him around.

and also he sleeps most of the day time and he is very pleasant when he sleeps

from your baby's brother age 7

Dear Birthmother,
Your baby is right beside me watching me write this note to you.

    He is the healthiest, happiest, smartest and most wanted baby (I think) in the whole world

We have enjoyed him so so so much these two months. Already I feel like he's been here at our house for a long time.

    I love his laugh and I love him, he's the sweetest baby.

        Lovingly,
        His adoptive sister

    Age 9 going on 10

Our last letter, from Cara Speedlin, age 11, who engages in ongoing visitation and other communication with her birthmother, demonstrates how children who are living with open adoption consider this to be "normal" adoption (as discussed further in *Children of Open Adoption*):

> Dear Birthmother (Liz),
>
> I think open adoption is very satisfying. I think this way of adoption is better than closed adoption because you know who gave birth to you and you at least know who your father is.
>
> Birthmother, I'm glad you chose open adoption. I remember the first time we met. Do you? I remember how much fun we had. You and Kenny were the greatest. I'm thankful that you named my half-sister after me.
>
> All these things could not have been possible without open adoption. I hope to continue to communicate with you.
>
> > Love,
> > Cara Elizabeth Speedlin
> > (age 11)

Recommended Reading

Arms, Suzanne, *Adoption: A Handful of Hope*, Berkeley, Celestial Arts, 1989 (originally published as *To Love and Let Go*)

Gritter, Jim, editor, *Adoption Without Fear*, San Antonio, Corona Publishing Co., 1989

Halverson, Kaye, with Karen M. Hess, *The Wedded Unmother*, Minneapolis, Augsburg Publishing House, 1980

Johnston, Patricia Irwin, *An Adoptor's Advocate*, Indianapolis, IN, Perspectives Press, 1984

_____, *Adopting After Infertility*, Fort Wayne, IN, Perspectives Press, 1992

_____ , *Taking Charge of Infertility*, Fort Wayne, IN, Perspectives Press, 1994

Kirk, David H. *Adoptive Kinship*, Toronto, Butterworth & Co., 1981

Kirk, David H., *Shared Fate: A Theory of Adoption and Mental Health*, New York, The Free Press, 1964

Lifton, Betty Jean, *Lost and Found*, New York, Harper & Row, 1988

Lindsay, Jeanne Warren, *Open Adoption: A Caring Option*, Buena Park, CA, Morning Glory Press, 1987

Lindsay, Jeanne Warren and Catherine Monserrat, *Adoption Awareness*, Buena Park, CA, Morning Glory Press, 1989

Melina, Lois Ruskai, *Raising Adopted Children*, New York, Harper & Row, 1986

Melina, Lois Ruskai and Sharon Kaplan Roszia, *The Open Adoption Experience*, New York, Harper Perennial, 1993

Menning, Barbara Eck, *Infertility: A Guide for the Childless Couple*, Englewood Cliffs, NJ, Prentice-Hall, Inc., 1977

Musser, Sandra Kay, *I Would Have Searched Forever*, Plainfield, NJ, Haven Books, 1979

Pannor, Reuben and Annette Baran, "Open Adoption As Standard Practice," *Child Welfare*, New York, Child Welfare League of America, Inc., Volume LXIII, Number 3, May-June 1984

Rappaport, Bruce, *The Open Adoption Book: A Guide to Making Adoption Work For You,* New York, MacMillan Publishing Co., 1992

Rillera, Mary Jo and Sharon Kaplan, *Cooperative Adoption*, Westminster, CA, Triadoption Publications, 1984

Roles, Patricia, *Saying Goodbye to Baby, Volume I: The Birthparent's Guide to Loss and Grief in Adoption; Volume II: A Counselor's Guide to Birthparent Loss and Grief in Adoption*, Washington, DC, Child Welfare League of America, Inc., 1989

Silber, Kathleen and Patricia Martinez Dorner, *Children of Open Adoption*, San Antonio, Corona Publishing Co., 1990

Sorosky, Arthur D., Annette Baran, and Reuben Pannor, *The Adoption Triangle*, San Antonio, Corona Publishing Co., 1989

Stephenson, Mary, *My Child is a Mother*, San Antonio, Corona Publishing Co., 1991

Verny, Thomas, M.D., with John Kelly, *The Secret Life of the Unborn Child*, New York, A Delta Book, 1981

Wishard, Laurie and William Wishard, *Adoption: The Grafted Tree*, San Francisco, Cragment, 1979

Books for Children

Girard, Linda Walvoord, *Adoption Is For Always*, Niles, IL, Albert Whitman & Co., 1986

Krementz, Jill, *How It Feels to be Adopted*, New York, Knopt, 1982

Lifton, Betty Jean, *I'm Still Me*, New York, Bantam Books, Inc., 1981

Livingston, Carole, *Why Was I Adopted?* Secaucus, NJ, Lyle Stuart, Inc., 1978

Nerlove, Evelyn, *Who is David?* New York, Child Welfare League of America, 1985

Silber, Kathleen and Debra Marks Parelskin, *My Special Family—A Children's Book About Open Adoption*, Orinda, CA, Open Adoption Press, 1994